HER MAJESTY'S PHILOSOPHERS

Alan Smith

Her Majesty's Philosophers
Alan Smith

Published 2013 by
Waterside Press
Sherfield Gables
Sherfield on Loddon
Hook, Hampshire
United Kingdom RG27 0JG

Telephone +44(0)1256 882250
E-mail enquiries@watersidepress.co.uk
Online catalogue WatersidePress.co.uk

ISBN 978-1-904380-95-5 (Paperback)
ISBN 978-1-908162-40-3 (Kindle/Epub ebook)
ISBN 978-1-908162-41-0 (Adobe ebook)

Cover design © 2013 Waterside Press. Design by www.gibgob.com.

Main UK distributor Gardners Books, 1 Whittle Drive, Eastbourne, East Sussex, BN23 6QH. Tel: +44 (0)1323 521777; sales@gardners.com; www.gardners.com

Cataloguing-In-Publication Data A catalogue record for this book can be obtained from the British Library.

Printed by CPI Group (UK) Ltd, Croydon, CR0 4YY.

e-book *Her Majesty's Philosophers* is available as an ebook and also to subscribers of Myilibrary, Dawsonera, ebrary, and Ebscohost.

Her Majesty's Philosophers

Alan Smith

✹ **WATERSIDE** PRESS

Contents

Acknowledgements

I owe a debt to the men who came to my classes and in exchange for my world let me into theirs. In a rather different way Mark Allen of South Texas College introduced me to the genre of Captivity Narratives and told everyone we met that I was 'distinguished'. Similarly, Jill Jones of Rollins College Florida and Kit Givan of the University of Central Oklahoma persuaded their universities to offer me scholarships and relentlessly promoted my work. At the *Guardian*, Peter Kingston and then Alice Woolley kept on accepting my articles and edited my words with good sense, dreamt up some extraordinary headlines and, finally, printed my picture. Debbie Kirby at the Ministry of Justice, always patient and sensible in her advice, had the knack of making me think again.

I am grateful to Bryan Gibson for wanting to publish this book, for his brisk, perceptive editing and, especially, for the surreal *Index* he has created.

About the Author

Alan Smith is a novelist whose columns for the *Guardian* introduced readers to several of the absorbing characters and true storylines in this book. A novelist, playwright and Northampton University lecturer as well as being a prison tutor, he empathises with life's failures, and as he explains in this book, Philosophy in prison may sound a strange permutation, but neither was that subject a regular degree choice for someone raised in the back streets of post-war Sheffield.

Her Majesty's Philosophers

Introduction

When the college rang and asked if I could do a few hours in the local prison I had no idea that another sort of reality was poised to seep into my head. Teaching in a prison seemed like an interesting idea and it sounded, too, as if there would be lots to write about. I knew that there was a strand of journalism which chiselled out stories from the day-to-day stuff that just happened and I was already planning to take notes.

I did one story for the *Times Educational Supplement* and then I was seduced away. *The Scotsman* wrote to me; they liked my piece in the TES and would I do something for their Education Section. I was off like a shot and for some months I was devoted to them. It was a bit like being a foreign correspondent, sending back news from a southern outpost. Then I sold a piece to *The Guardian*. One thing had led to another and there I was telling people that I was a journalist.

'Oh, *The Guardian* actually,' I would say.

I've now been writing for that newspaper, about prison and one or two other things, for the past ten years and it's a lovely system. Ten years, and I've never set foot in the office. I write the article, email it, they print it and put the money in my account. No need for me ever to get out of bed; I could just make it up. Well, no, given the things that have happened in my classroom, in the prison I don't think that I could have made it up. There have been times when I've thought that the men might be making stuff up, feeding me prison fictions just to see how far my credulity and *The Guardian's* could be stretched. But no, of course they wouldn't ... would they?

I had been writing and publishing prison stories for three years before anyone official realised what I was doing. I wasn't being secretive, I hadn't set out to be devious. I had just got on with it. When they discovered me the people at the Home Office (since 2007 prisons have come under the Ministry of Justice) were slightly put out. In fact one chap became mildly hysterical, a bit aggressive, at the thought of unsupervised stories in the national press. When I stopped to think about it I could see his point of view. As far as he was concerned I was a journalist who had sneaked in under dubious pretences. It is, so they tell me, not easy for journalists to have access to prisons and there I was wandering the place with my own set of keys and a winning smile.

In fact there was nothing at all to be nervous about because I had my own rules of conduct which were not really journalistic at all. I never published anything without showing it first to anyone who was mentioned and I always changed or omitted anything with which they felt uncomfortable. From the outset I made up my mind to be relentlessly positive about all the people I met. People in prison are too vulnerable, too much the sitting duck.

Our attitudes towards prisoners are habitually negative, many people think of prison as being the place where the demons are kept.

'My son's in prison.'

'Oh that's nice.'

You just don't hear it. There is, however, a positive story to tell and in prison some men achieve much that is to be celebrated and admired. When these self-imposed restraints failed there was Peter Kingston and later Alice Woolley at *The Guardian* who edited out my excesses and, for the last few years, the people at what is now the Ministry of Justice who saved me from blundering about. I always had the uncomfortable feeling that they were taking pity on me. Above all they were calm and sensible and knew completely how to get their own way by pointing out what a fool I was about to make of myself.

These restraints have left me with a lot of material in my notebooks which I have not used, some of it I shall never use. But, there is a case for telling a more complete, a more balanced story for which a book, this book, is a more appropriate setting than the snapshot of a short newspaper column. Many stories are too long, too complicated to fit into the 600 words I have as a journalist. I also have the desire to tell my story, to tell the truth or as near to it as I can manage.

We were all busily making truths which made prison life livable. There are, though, those of us who are self-consciously setting out to be storytellers. We might make things up or we might shape the truth into a better telling. We do not conspire with each other, or even simply with ourselves, to make up things which are false but story telling sometimes has a life, an impetus, of its own.

The experience of prison has inevitably found its way into my writing. I have written plays and novels where, whether or not I initially intended it, prison has intruded itself. This feeling of being taken over is accentuated when I write stories for newspapers or magazines. If I write more words than my editor has asked me for my story is cut to size. If I write fewer then my fee is reduced. The constraints are unavoidable and of course being paid by the word is an effective and humbling discipline. A little while ago an editor telephoned me to ask me for a couple more centimetres. I think that what I conjured up was truthful, at least not wilfully false, but I had about ten minutes to do it. This is the kind of crude treatment to which writers and their texts become accustomed; it is also an ever present reminder that when I write I am making an artefact, as surely as the life in my classroom is an artefact, and that the quality of that artefact need not have much to do with truth.

These experiences have made me wary of eye-witness accounts, narrative accounts which claim to be telling the truth. Those of us who attempt to extract propositional knowledge from storytelling need to be aware not only of the profile and situation of the teller but of the editorial and commercial pressures which inevitably exist and which may be beyond even the teller's influence. Because of these pressures it may well be that the narratives we read are not sourced unambiguously in their author; they may have been remade in response to the commercial or ideological ambitions of an editor or a publisher. We have to consider a range of narratological judgements: point of view, the reliability of the narrative voice, genre and so on.

As a journalist I have a responsibility to tell the truth but as a writer of short stories, plays, novels, I have developed attitudes to the truth which are not altogether scientific. Scientific truth seems to me to be relatively simple: something either is the case or it is not. Scientific truth is verified by a system of investigation which is itself testable and open. In my true stories, and I wish to claim that they are all true stories, it might be that the dialogue was never said in quite the words which I quote or that there is an exaggeration here, an understatement there, perhaps time has been rearranged. I set out to tell truths about prison but the limits of my medium have driven me to employ the devices of fiction.

As well as being as watchful as any prudent person would be in a prison I am also watchful in that nosey-parkerish way, that intrusive way that writers need to have. If a prisoner tells me something about a book they are reading or about the best way to rob a supermarket, I always press them for detail and I know that when they say: 'What do you wanna know that for,' I can disarm them by saying: 'Well, you know I'm a writer don't you?'

And then, generally, it needs a dose of Valium to shut them up. Most people, and especially convicts, will tell you anything if they think that you will write about them. I have notebooks full of stories which can never be told if only on the grounds of taste and decency. The men know that I am always on the look-out for dialogue, anecdote, incident and sometimes it occurs to me that they might make things up just to be obliging. Not only to be obliging, but to be thought well of. It might also be the case that someone might make things up out of a sense of fun or mischief or, as I have already said, just to see how far my credulity can be stretched. None of this worries me. When I am sitting there on the Lifer Wing listening to someone's thrilling adventures I am not too bothered whether the stories are true or not and to be honest I seem to lose my grip on morality as well. Is this shocking? No, of course not; a good story well told is what I really enjoy and what's more it is something which I can easily recognise and appreciate.

The truth, on the other hand, presents me with all kinds of difficulties and raises all sorts of troublesome questions. I feel quite secure about scientific truths but once I get into moral, social or emotional truth things quickly become less certain, more about what I feel than what I know. Luckily I am not engaged in methodical, scientific research. I am engaged in producing primary texts, stories about captivity and I know that this process is subject to pressures which go far beyond a concern for truth. I am not unconcerned with truth but I have to acknowledge that my concern for impact, dramatic effectiveness, the aesthetic of form and language are often my foremost considerations.

Amongst prisoners the man who can tell a good story is highly valued. Rex was the best storyteller I have ever heard. He came into my class when he had done 12 years of a 16 year sentence. He was an armed robber and had all the innocent self-confidence which is common in the armed robber community. He was a well-spoken, good looking man who kept himself nicely groomed and dressed smartly. He was polite, pleasant and good natured. You had to see past the armed robber part of him. Except that he would not let you. He loved to tell armed robbery stories. What was stunningly shrewd was that he never told them directly about armed robbery; his narratives were indirect, elusive, the main event, like Godot, was always offstage. If Rex were being chased by the police it was neither the chase nor the police which was significant. It was the ploughed field.

> 'I drove until I just ran out of road and I was out of the car and legging it across this field. It was a ploughed field and it was wet and I couldn't run. I was sinking in and pulling my legs out and running in slow motion and getting nowhere, it was like a cartoon, and I thought I'm fucked they're gonna get me easy. And then I looked behind and there was a line of Old Bill behind me all doing like me all treacled up in the field and we did this slow motion chase until I got to the hedge and I was away. And I hid in this lake and it was freezing and ...'

Rex didn't give a hoot about anything but the Charlie Chaplin effect of the mud. He was the least reliable narrator in the world. He completely misrepresented the world of armed robbery. He told stories about his mother-in-law, about his wife, about his disguises. Rex brought us together and made us think better of him.

When we reflect on Rex's use of detail we can see that it is highly selective and intended for a particular purpose. When Rex told us about his mother-in-law finding a bullet down the back of the settee he told us about her hairdo, the pattern on the cushion covers, the coffee table on which she carefully placed the bullet. I used to hang on his every word and believed completely in everything he said. Rex's stories helped to establish him in the prison; he showed us a version of himself which was made in the process of storytelling.

The truth is, at best, an odd business and I know that prisons are places where stories of all sorts flourish. I have relied on my notebooks, my newspaper articles as well as reflection and memory. In class I always had my notebook with me and I jotted down anything which came my way. If the men were improving on reality or making up a particularly pungent phrase so that they could sneak into the paper then I have to admit to being pretty well defenceless. I made a point of believing everything and I kept on telling them, 'If you say it's true, then as far as I'm concerned, it is true. I don't mind if you make a dick of me. Why should I?'

1

A Willing Fool

I had expected that getting into the prison would be complicated but, on the phone, Jean was quite matter of fact. 'I'll meet you at the gate,' she said. 'Just tell the officers to give me a call in Education. Bring some ID.'

I showed the officer my passport. 'Education?' he said, flat faced, serious. There were four of them, behind the armoured glass, white shirts, black ties and epaulettes. Their calm deadpan made me even more nervous; they could take me or leave me. Then, there Jean was, across the air lock, behind the second heavy metal gate. She was a tiny dark woman and I thought, 'How can she protect me?' I could see her talking to the officer on her side of the door. She pointed at me, stabbing her finger and laughing. The officer on my side gestured me through and I heard the sharp click that released the lock. I shook Jean's tiny hand.

'Got to be quick,' she said, 'the men are a bit early.'

There were more gates, five of them, and a quick glimpse of lawn and flowerbeds, tall metal fences topped with wire, a brick cell block, numbered windows. Then we were, suddenly, in a corridor full of noise and men. How could Jean protect me? What use would she be? She clapped her hands, 'Come on, come on then, let's have you in your classrooms.' Like a bossy middle-class infants teacher with some raggy-arsed kids.

The corridor emptied as she chivvied and nagged her way along. 'You're in here,' she said to me in the same brisk way. 'You'll be alright with this group, they're nice.' Nice? Why were they locked up if they were nice? 'Dean,' she said and a dark, good looking man, about 30-years-of-age, stood up from his desk and gave her a Hugh Grant smile. 'Look after Alan will you?' And she was gone.

'You the teacher mate?'

'That's what Jean says.'

'Yeah, she's a bit scary when she's on one.'

And everything was suddenly normal, just like that, with Dean pulling me into a rueful male alliance against the bossy women.

I don't know why I did it but it was the best move I could have made: I shook everyone's hand and we introduced ourselves: Mr. Williams, Mr. Knight, Mr. Ericson… and I asked if they would mind if we used Christian names. It was a good way of ridding myself of authority. There is, in prison, a massive distorting weight of authority pressing onto every relationship and I knew, straightaway, that not only did I dislike it but that I didn't have it in me to join in the exercise. On the one hand I wasn't strong enough to pull it off and on the other I wasn't insecure enough to need it. It was one of those very rare moments when you see something clearly.

There were six of them and we sat around in a circle and talked about Hamlet. 'You know,' said Michael,' this Ophelia, she strikes me as the sort of heroine that Jane Austen might have written about.' Of course she was. Why hadn't I thought of that? But someone was already talking about the tragic dimension that just wasn't there in Austen. Except in a domestic sense, someone else said. And there I was, out of my depth, delighted, not believing my luck. I was only with that group for a month, until their regular teacher came back, but they turned me inside out.

Prison is where the demons are isn't it: degenerate, violent, predatory? Yet here I was in the heart of it with Jane Austen and Shakespeare.

I was ready for my cup of tea at break but Michael made a bee-line for me and I could see that there was something that had to be said, something that he wanted to make clear. 'I am not,' he said, 'a criminal.' I could think of nothing sensible to say. I certainly wasn't going to tell him that he was; I could see what eight or nine years of prison gym had done for him.

'I am a decent person. I do not cheat or rob or tell lies. I am a murderer.'

'Well, that's all right then,' said Dean, and a very strange moment passed.

This was 1998 before it was usual for cells to have electricity and certainly before in-cell television was commonplace. Men like those in my Hamlet group would read their sentences away: a book a day, more at weekends when there was lots of bang up.

'Everyone should do prison,' Dean told me. 'It's a very revealing thing. When you're on your own in the dark and it's three o'clock in the morning and you can't sleep and you've got years of it ahead of you, that's when you find out about yourself. That's when you find out who you are.'

'No, I don't want to do that, Dean.'

'You should, you should.'

He made me see, straightaway, how dreadful prison was and how absurd any talk about the softness of the system: the populist, suburban rubbish about holiday camps and criminals doing better than ordinary hard-working people and so on. I was already, on my first morning, developing a preference for robbers and villains and addicts; wickedness and vulnerability seeming all at once to be more attractive than the mean spirited moral penny-pinching of the lower middle-class. Of course all of this dissolved the minute I talked to my wife. At lunch she gave me the pitying look of someone who had heard this kind of thing before. She thought that I was off my head.

Gwen, who taught literacy in the prison, put it like this: 'I dread my daughter coming home with someone like Dean. I mean, he's such a nice chap, he'd just charm you into submission wouldn't he? He's lovely. And then he'd get into some scrape and he'd be doing seven years again and everybody would think that he was a hero for not grassing on his mates and he'd write lovely letters and pass his A-Levels and it would be just awful.'

It was Dean who explained the system to me. I had been surprised to meet men doing life sentences alongside those serving a few months. We were a Category C prison and I had assumed that lifers, for example, would be in high security regimes. In fact the system is more fluid than that. There are relatively few Cat-A prisoners. These are people who present significant problems of safety and security more so than Cat-B prisoners who have nevertheless been convicted of serious offences. Men, for example, who have been convicted of murder will begin their sentences in a Cat-A establishment and depending on the offence serve part of their tariff in that regime before progressing to Cat-B and beyond. They might then be re-classified as Cat-C and serve some years amongst a more varied population before being assessed as suitable for Cat-D, open conditions, and then release on licence, possibly under a resettlement scheme.

As well as making progress men might find themselves moving backwards in the system. A man might infringe the terms of his licence and find himself back in Cat-B. Making progress in the system is, naturally, a major preoccupation, and a source of anxiety for most of the men.

I could see why the officers might become quite negative about the prisoners, after all some of them were quite difficult, and equally I could see why the prisoners didn't think too well of the people who banged them up at half-past-eight, searched them, wrote reports on them and so on. None of this touched me and I watched and stared and took it all in.

Being a teacher left me nowhere to stand, made me an agreeable hypocrite moving on the shifting sands of the prison. It began to dawn on me that this was a large part of my value: that I had nothing to do with prison. I had the opportunity to bring with me into the place a bubble of the ordinary world and keep it intact for us to live in, intact, without authority and without making judgements. My values were a world apart from the values of the prison. My starting point, that people were good, was enough to mark me out as a fool, a fool that I was willing to be. These contradictions have never been resolved and as the first weeks went by and I met more and more of the men, more of the officers it was difficult not to agree with everyone's contradictory opinions.

For weeks I assumed that Jim in the Education Office was just that: the bloke in the office, someone who went home for his tea.

'You silly bugger,' Helen told me, 'he killed his wife.'

'Well,' I said, 'he seems a nice enough bloke to me.'

'He is,' she said.

Jim was in his sixties, an engineer with a lifetime of directing major construction projects behind him.

'Before this, Alan, I don't think that I'd ever had so much as a parking ticket. Then at 56 I get a life sentence.'

Anybody doing a maths qualification came to Jim. In fact the son of one of the officers got a lot of help from Jim with his A-Level. Distance learning, of course. He worked in the office with Phil. Phil was doing English in my A-Level group and everybody took the piss out of his thick Brummie accent. He had had a firm which imported furniture from the Far East and had rented out a space in one of his containers to someone who was a bit dodgy and now, four years later, it had all gone: house, business, car, wife. Not even the officers could see the sense in locking him up and they let him have a cell up on the Lifer Wing where the inmates were a bit older, a bit more stable and respectable.

Phil had struck up an unlikely friendship with Noel who was doing an enormous sentence for armed robbery and they were planning how they could clean and decorate Noel's new cell. The preoccupations of many of the men were with these sorts of ordinary, domestic things. Most of all, for men like these, there were standards of respectability for which they strived, which made life possible.

2

In Your Dreams

When Les turned up he had a thin, scraped air about him. He was a small, skinny Welshman who looked as though he had been too cold for far too long. Les had low expectations of the future:

'If I get my parole, I'd like to have a dog. Be nice that.'

A couple of the other men had sent him along to show me some writing that he had done. He had been watching some sparrows out of his cell window and had made up a rough ironic love story about them. It sounds a bit soft, but it was lovely writing, a real tough guy tour de force. Les had been in jail, at Her Majesty's pleasure, since he was 16. He had started off in YOI and came to us after seven years in Dartmoor.

'I was really scared, you know, but my Mam and Dad they've been there for me all the time. When I was first in I tried to get my Mam to bring me some drugs in. I can't believe it now. She said: "If you love me, Les' you'll never ask me that again." I was a bit of a prick wasn't I?'

'I'm not a big bloke, Alan, and I knew I'd get it. First week in YOI and this big guy comes into my pad and he says to me, "I'll be round to see you Friday when you get your canteen." I was shittin' myself. I thought, no fuck this. If I let this get started, I'll never see the end of it. Friday comes, and I'm waiting for this guy and he comes into my pad. I was shittin' myself. "What you got for me?" he says. Christ Al, he was humongous. I made myself do it. "I've got fuck all for you," right in his face, "so fuck off." You know what? He fucked off. I was a bit lucky mind.'

Les palled up with Matt, a smart North Londoner, a really tough looking bullet of a man in his mid-twenties who would arrive for class with books under his arm and dead keen.

'When you're in prison you get clean, get fit, get some education. That's what I told Big.'

'Hello,' said Big and we shook hands.

To get called Big in jail you really do have to be beefy. There are high standards of beefiness. Big never came to my class, he always went to Carole for Sociology and he was quite an asset. In fact he became our hero. Carole had been talking about homosexuality and had presented it as being at least morally neutral. One thing led to another and then one man, enraged, was on his feet and making for her. Big just stood in his way.

'It was absurd,' Carole said, afterwards, 'he just couldn't get round Big, you know the size of him.'

He could have hit Big, but who in their right mind would? Every time he tried to get at Carole, Big just took half a step to the side and wouldn't let him. Never raised his hands, just stood there. The bloke ran out of steam in the end, he just deflated and sat down. Even so it made me think of the effrontery of going into a prison and asking the men to read poetry and settle down with a book. But that, of course was just another lesson in how prison was ordinary, not especially wicked, and when I managed to step away from my prejudices and think about it, much, much more pleasant than the schools and colleges I had worked in.

In the days when I had been a schoolteacher I had always been rather ill at ease with telling people what to do; sit up straight, get your books out, do this, do that. I mean, why should they? Happily, all that sort of thing was out of the question on the inside. Well, it was for me. For the women teachers it was different. I was amazed at the levels of compliance they achieved by being martinets. The inmates called them 'Miss' and gave in to what I saw at first as outrageous tyranny:

'I am not having you come into Education in shorts, absolutely not.'

'You do not run in the corridor.'

'Excuse me, I think that I'm speaking? Thank you. That's better.'

But, of course, everyone knew that their teachers would always go the extra mile for them, that they would organize books and videos and tuition.

Gerry was a good example of this. He was new in Cat-C and he came to one of my literature classes. He looked dreadful; he looked ill and defeated as though gripped by a desperate, slow motion panic that had pulled the flesh from his bones. When he spoke he was hesitant, apologetic. He told me about how he had done something terrible and that it was only when he was years into his life sentence that what he had done had suddenly struck him.

'Before, I didn't care. When I was sentenced, lifed off, I didn't care. I sat in the cells at the court, read the paper, had a smoke. The officer said: "You alright?" "Yeah," I said, "why shouldn't I be?" that's what I was like. Then, years in, I had a nervous breakdown. Proper breakdown. It dawned on me what I'd done. Bit strange really.'

Gerry was quiet in class but if I asked him directly about something he would always be thoughtful and sharp. We had been reading Larkin's poem, Water, 'If I were called in / to construct a religion / I should make use of water' and Gerry said,

'I did a certificate in Theology a couple of years back. Don't see how I'll ever do anything with that do you?'

And then he told me about his half-finished Open University degree, abandoned years ago.

'You should get back to it.'

'How can I? Too late now.'

'What were you doing?'

'Social sciences.'

'Do you want to do it?'

'Too late, Alan, left it too late.'

I saw Jean at break and asked her if there was anything to be done. She picked up the phone. About half-an-hour later she came and interrupted us.

'Gerry?'

He looked up like a surprised ghost.

'I want you. Come on, come with me.'

When he came back he had the bewildered look of a man being blown before a storm.

'I'm doing OU,' he said.

'Starting when?'

'I've started. I don't know how she's done it.'

'It's best to keep out of her way Ges.'

Gerry vanished into his OU degree, went off to Carole's sociology class, got some computer skills and read everything. Before his degree was completed he went off to a Cat-D, open prison, got a job on the out. He was still glum, still saying: 'I've got no illusions, you know, who's going to have anything to do with me?' A couple of years later Carole was invited to his graduation. He got a First.

I could see that Les and Matt were plotting something, 'What's going on then?'

'You don't want to know, Al.'

'Oh.'

'Just planning for when I get my D,' said Les.

'I said I'd buy him a present,' said Matt. 'I've got a few bob.'

'Don't tell me, I don't want to know.'

'Course you don't.'

'He's gonna buy me a prostitute,' said Les.

'I'll buy you two if you like.'

'Would you?'

'Course I would.'

'Two prostitutes.'

Les's face had gone a bit dreamy.

'That'll be alright Al, don't you reckon?'

He had been away for at least 12 years.

'Do you think that two will be enough?' I asked.

He looked a bit thoughtful. 'You taking the piss are you?'

I left them to it.

'Let me know when you get your first leave,' I could hear Matt saying, 'I'll book a hotel.'

Within weeks most of my first group, the Hamlet group, had melted away. Someone had been released, someone else off on a course to do with sentence progression, someone off to Cat-D. I found it odd. There had been a feeling of intimacy in the group and now men were missing but not missed. Everyone faded quickly in the bustle of getting through sentences and the stages that sentences fell into. One of the guys said: 'There are no friends in prison just lots of people you know, lots of acquaintances.'

But then there was David, another pal of Les's. We were standing in the corridor and I said to him: 'You'll be going home soon won't you David?'

'No, not now, not for a bit.' He'd had a four year sentence and been perfect; he should have been away on licence.

'What's happened?'

'Fucked up didn't I.'

Les butted in. He was staring hard at David.

'I tested positive,' he said.

'You'd have been in the shit,' David said.

'So, he said it was him that had spiked my tea, that I was an innocent victim.'

'They'd have knocked you back to a D Cat,' David said. He turned to me. 'He'd have had years to do on top, being a lifer. They'd have had him back in B Cat. Fucking ridiculous. Me? They only took a few months off me.'

I don't suppose that after David's release they ever saw each other again. Not long after Les made it to his D. I hope he did okay with the prostitutes.

Her Majesty's Philosophers

3

Prison Craft and Long John Silver

My first few months in prison were disconcerting. Quite early on I did a course in Prison Craft. Prison Craft sounded very odd to me but the two officers who ran it made their points in a worryingly persuasive way. Entering a prison as a teacher, especially a part-time teacher means that you bring in with you all the ordinary attitudes of a respectable middle-class life and far from being alert to differences the assumptions of the 'out' continue seamlessly into the inside. Someone might say to you: 'Alan, could you just drop this into the post for me? And I might ordinarily say: 'Yes, of course.' Reflection might tell you that this could be problematic but as ordinary people with ordinary lives this is the kind of reflection that we don't go in for. 'Then,' said the officer, 'you might find yourself posting quite a few letters or bringing in a bit of chocolate or "a little parcel my mate on the out's got for my birthday," and then you're so far into deceiving Security that they'll have you doing all sorts.'

I was a bit disbelieving about this. Sounds melodramatic, I thought, but I did make a point of explaining in class just how respectable I was.

'You can't tell me that,' I would say, like a startled virgin, 'I'm a respectable middle-aged man.'

I would bang on about how much I detested drugs, how I believed in law and order and following the rules. I always called the officers, 'officers' and never 'screws' and always demonstrated that I was on first name terms with them and that some of them were my friends. Prison Craft!

I was still shocked, though, when teachers were caught out: the middle-aged lady who did the soft toys class, the new basic skills teacher, the elderly Christian lady who helped out in the chapel. I'm still not sure about the details of any of these instances because Security can be surprisingly discrete and humane at times. I was only asked once to post a letter, a birthday card for Rory's dad, and I refused. I felt rotten about it and years later, writing this, I still do. Rory was a nice bloke doing a first sentence for something to do with drugs and I was sure that he was perfectly genuine and had asked a favour as an ordinary person might ask. He was an ordinary person, not a criminal by any stretch of the imagination, no-one would mind having him home for tea. But, I told him, no, and we were both embarrassed and, I think, somehow ashamed. Prison has a dreadful, poisoning effect.

Attempting to avoid this effect is one of the reasons why people take sides. It is easy and understandable for an officer to say: 'Ninety-five per cent of these bastards are just scum,' and for prisoners to say the same thing back. There had been some sort of confrontation between one of the officers and a prisoner and Matt had stepped in, taken the guy away and talked to him, made him see sense. The Principal Officer on the wing had wanted to write on Matt's record that he had, 'come to the help of an officer in danger,' thinking that it might do Matt a bit of good, I suppose. It was a thank you.

Matt was outraged, 'I don't want that in my record. I wasn't helping that bastard. Help them, you must be joking, fucking disgrace. I was helping my mate.'

When he told me this I was non-plussed and faced with this bewilderment of mine he took time to explain things to me. Then, I told him how well everyone had behaved: he had intervened, his pal had listened, the officer didn't press things, the PO wanted to say thanks.

'Fucking bastards.'

But, nevertheless something had happened and someone like me, so out of place, needed to be there to point it out. I could see that my colleagues were doing the same sort of thing. We were coming into the prison trailing clouds of respectability: civilians, not part of the game.

Education was and is the politest part of the prison. The women teachers are referred to as 'Miss', and then, after a little while in class, a few weeks maybe, people begin to use first names. Male teachers set their own, blokey, parameters, first names are usual from the outset.

When a new man comes into my class, I shake his hand and call him Mr. Whatever and ask him if he minds using first names. This is not quite so simple as it seems. What I am doing is importing some outside behaviour into the inside. This is how I might well behave on the outside and it begins to set normal habits of behaviour for social relations between normal adult men. I am, too, ridding myself of some of the authority that a prisoner might expect to encounter in prison and I am offering him a little bit of the authority that choosing implies. I am not sneaking up on the guys in doing this; I tell them, straightforwardly, why we shake hands in my class, why we speak to each other as we do. This does not come as news to them but taking the time and trouble to make these things explicit makes the value system of my respectability a little bit more worthy of consideration and that consideration speaks to notions of identity and self-worth, both of which can be a little bit ephemeral inside prison.

It started in that first Hamlet class with that stroke of good luck when I shook Dean's hand. I've been shaking hands ever since and everyone who comes into my room gets a handshake when they arrive and when they leave. We always thank each other for the morning that we have had.

In the past I had, at times, been a schoolteacher and for me one of the most grating aspects of schools was the authority that I was expected to exercise over my pupils. One of my first thoughts in the prison was that my authority over men who were bigger, fitter, faster and younger than me might turn out to be a little bit theoretical. What was I going to do: lines, detention, get in touch with their mums, clip round the ear? Matt in particular got very annoyed with me:

'Come on Al, use your authority. You need to assert yourself here.'

'No Matthew, I have no authority at all. It's your class; you're all grown men, why should you listen to me? I don't want any rights over you. All I can do is offer you things.'

And there they were, listening. 'Should we have a quick look at page 38? What do you think?'

They knew what I was up to, of course they did. We all conspired to make it possible for me to be in charge, well, partly in charge, without there being an intrusive hierarchy in the room. It was all a bit two-faced because I relied on the fact that, mostly, I knew more than they did and I could play the cultural conjurer, pulling clever rabbits out of the hat. I was doing my stuff one Thursday afternoon, reading *Hamlet* and giving a commentary on the text when Maurice stopped me. Maurice was built out of a series of cubes, a bit like Mr. Strong but stronger.

'You don't think we can read this for ourselves do you? ... You think we're thick.'

He stopped me dead and we looked at each other. The class sat back and watched, interested.

'You're right,' I said, 'got that one wrong didn't I?'

'Yeah you did, didn't you?'

'Sorry.'

'You should be careful about thinking people are thick.'

'Don't rub it in Maurice. Just read it if you want to.'

'Don't know if I do.'

'Oh for God's sake.'

Then, he read it; read it beautifully in a buttery Black Country accent. In fact, given that Shakespeare came from the Midlands it was how he might have read it himself. Try it, if you can do the accent, it sounds great.

I didn't realise at the time how much good I had done myself; Maurice had had a little bite at me and I had had a little bite back. After that he always came and sat at my side and read a lot and I didn't have to worry about authority for quite a while. He was the sort of man who came with his own quiet atmosphere. Ginge got me on my own one day.

'You know what he's in for don't you?'

'None of my business Ginge.'

But Ginge thought that it was and he was obviously enormously impressed and bursting with the story.

'He was in a big fight in a pub, real Wild West punch up and at the end he was last man standing. Everything in the pub smashed to little bits, so he gets himself a drink and stands at the bar. The police come and try to get him out and he says, "No", he's just having a peaceful drink and the coppers didn't fancy the job at all and so in the end they just threw a great big police Alsatian in. Maurice killed it. Bare hands, just killed it. Two years he's got. Fucking doggicide Al, that's what he's in for.'

When I saw Maurice again I couldn't resist the odd remark about careers in animal welfare that he might consider and there was a bleak second or two when I thought that I might have gone too far. He gave me a little smile, rather rueful, rather modest. He was released a couple of weeks before his

GCSE exams and he promised faithfully to go to his local FE College to sit them. I don't suppose he did.

Prisons are quite special places for some people. They are a sort of time out from the hurly burly where some things become uniquely possible. Matt took as his mantra, 'Get clean, get fit, get some education', seriously. There was no ulterior motive in Matt's focus on education. He never saw it as a career move; he steadfastly did all the useless 'fluffy' subjects: Literature, Drama, Philosophy, History. He took the English Literature as far as A-Level. There had been a biggish group coming along to class, going through the texts and joining in the discussions. In fact I was surprised at just how much interest there was in really close reading, sometimes from guys who couldn't actually read. Only Matt and Adrian did the exam (Adrian foolishly let it slip that his local paper had denounced him as a 'Dealer in Death' and so he had acquired an unfortunate nickname). At the end of the last paper they stood up and, solemnly, shook hands with each other and then with me.

'I never thought I'd do that.'

'No, never.'

It left me a bit shocked; I hadn't realised what a mountain we'd been climbing.

Matt was due for release before the results came out but I was sure that he had at least, at the very least, passed.

'What are you going to do then?' I asked him. 'You could do something at college; get a job.'

'Fuck off, Alan,' he told me. 'A job? Some poxy minimum wage job? Listen, if I get up the motorway to Oxford or Cambridge with a carful of drugs for the posh kids I can make 40,000 quid a week, eight grand a day. Course I'm gonna get a job.'

There wasn't a lot to be said. Except that I found myself saying: 'Well, for God's sake, just take care that you don't get caught. You don't want to come back in here do you? You get caught again and you'll get an enormous sentence, won't you? Well, won't you?'

What was becoming of me? This wasn't what I should have been saying. I knew that. I should have been telling him about the evil of his ways, counselling virtue and hard work but there I was, committed to him getting away with it. He hadn't talked me into this, there hadn't been any effort to seduce me onto the Dark Side but I had been listening to lots of stories, lots of accounts of criminal adventure all told from an intensely personal point of view. When there's a villain in a film: *The Italian Job, The Thomas Crown Affair, Rififi* or in a novel like *Day Of The Jackal* isn't there always a part of us that wants the bad guy to get away with it? When a crime narrative streams out from the gangster's point of view or there is a first person account from a hit man or a pirate, don't you just want the respectable world to crumble, the cops to fail? Does anyone at all dislike Long John Silver? Perhaps it's just me, perhaps I'm easily led.

From where I was, sitting inside the Leviathan of state education, crime can look a lot like freedom. In crime there is no admin, no report writing, tax-declaring, no bureaucracy to serve. On the other hand there is prison.

'Listen Al, you come to work, you get your money and then you give away a third of it in tax. Alright, I have to come into prison from time-to-time, pay my dues.'

I was learning that prison is ordinary. Not only was it an expectable occurrence in someone's life but the place itself had long passages of just being ordinary in its routines and perspectives. Every time that I say to someone that I teach in a prison there is a reaction: is it dangerous, is it violent, nasty, sordid? I suppose that it can be at times but most of all it is ordinary and most prisoners are, mostly, ordinary. Or at least this is how it begins to seem. From a teacher's point of view prison can be quite pleasant. In the prison where I work there are more than 600 men of whom there are rarely more than 50 in Education at any one time. These men are, with the odd exception, probably the most motivated and in some cases the most intelligent people in the establishment. Men who really do want to learn to read and write, someone racing through computer qualifications so that he can keep up with his grand-daughter or learning arithmetic at 30-odd are the best pupils any teacher could have.

4

Absolute Scratch

Sharon ran the computer section and so she often had men from the whole range of ability at the same time. It was one of the quietest places in the prison. In any of the computer rooms there they would be rows of quiet faces smooth with concentration. When I went in there, just to have a nose around, a couple of the guys from my class gave me a brief smile then got straight back into what they were doing. I was more used to bust ups about Aristotle or how do we know if there is really a cup on the table. None of that nonsense here.

'This,' said Sharon, and she obviously thought that I was barmy, 'is focused on the individual, hardly any group dynamic at all. Some of the men find this a very safe environment where they can work at their own pace. We have to be careful not to overdo it though, it can be isolating. One man had terrible exam nerves, you know, sweating, palpitations. We can't let ourselves be too target driven. He comes in now just for the chance to learn something.'

But she did set some pretty formidable targets. There were guys who came into the computer room who couldn't read and the great bonus for them was that they did get that individual attention. She told me about Max, one of the orderlies, who was using the Shannon Trust's Toe-by-Toe literacy scheme to teach another of the inmates to read.

'The reading and the word-processing are emerging together. He's getting more and more confidence and it's carrying over into his Basic Skills class. Another man was doing Computer Literacy and Information Technology (CLAIT); it was the first certificate he'd ever had. Do you know, he phoned home to tell his wife.'

An important element, in Sharon's opinion, was to find the right kind of orderly. The standard courses in the prison went up to CLAIT Plus but sometimes men moved on to Dreamweaver, Fireworks and Flash and it was hard for the teachers to keep up with them.

'But', she said, 'I've marked Sue's card and when she's doing inductions she headhunts any new inmates who might have useful skills. Some of them, you know, are computer professionals with really advanced skills that it would be foolish not to use. But I'm really very cagey about my orderlies; their conduct with the other men is at least as important as the technical stuff. One of them, a couple of years ago now, he'd been a gym orderly, huge he was, had to turn sideways to get through the door. There was a bit of a row one day and he just stood over these two men and suggested they apologise to each other and shake hands. It wasn't because he was big, it was because he was calm. When someone said that they couldn't do something he would say, "Yeah, well, neither could I six months ago." It was a terrible blow when they released him.'

She sent me to have a word with Alex.

'I couldn't do anything, not a thing. Thought a mouse was something for the cat. I've got 14 grandchildren and they can all do computers, so now that I can do it, well, that's a point of contact isn't it? My eldest grandson's been telling me all about his work and my daughter, she's a school secretary, she's starting European Computer Driving Licence (ECDL) so she's doing it the same time as me. I said to them, look, I'm 60 next year and if I can do it anyone can do it. And I'm doing my GCSE English; couldn't write a proper letter when I came in here. I do stories for my grandkids, just little stories. Wouldn't have done any of this if I hadn't been unlucky enough to come to jail.'

Andy, the maths lecturer had a computer group in the room next door. Yeah, well,' he said to me, 'if you hadn't done sums for 20 years you'd be a bit rusty.' Andy could get very assertive when he was defending his students and he defended them all the time. 'It's not that these guys in numeracy are thick, anything but, they might just have missed out at school, anyway, they're a bit leery of education in general. Fred and Robert over there,' he pointed to two hunched figures, 'I kind of seduced them into computers.'

Robert sat up straight, turned round. 'You what? What seduction? You know what, I was frogmarched up to the office, he made me sign up. I went back after and took myself off the list, so he frogmarches me again, "Get this guy's name down." Like being arrested,' he smiled. 'Should've done it years ago.' In three weeks I can create a document, type a poem, save it, print it. First one's just gone off to the Koestler competition.'

Fred said, 'Yeah, it was one of the guys on the wing got me into it, word-of-mouth. But I was scared as well. My first class, it was nerve-wracking. "Take a seat," says Andy. Absolute scratch. There I was: keyboard, mouse and not a clue. Then you just get drawn through it. When I first looked in I saw all the machines, saw all the printers going, all the lads typing away. I thought, I don't want to make a pratt of myself.'

'But then,' said Walter, giving us the tooth-free smile, 'he saw an old pratt like me doing it.'

'Yeah', said Fred, 'I thought if he could do it anybody could.'

'People forget,' chipped in Walter again, 'they think that you just get youngsters in here but they're wrong. Old people come to prison as well. People like you Al.'

5

Droppers-In

At this early stage of my prison career the Education Department had its classrooms along one of the main corridors of the prison. This gave us quite an exciting life. If an alarm went off officers would run, full tilt in response; sometimes a man in trouble would have to be escorted past the classrooms and everything would be locked down. Most intriguingly, though, it meant that we were exposed to droppers-in, men going from one part of the prison to another would put their heads round the door to say hello to a friend or, as I got to know more people, to me. One day it was Big.

'Hiya Big,' I said, 'how's it going?'

'Fine, Al, fine. There's no place like jail.' Then he was off before we'd really got going with the song.

I made a point of trying to seduce all the droppers-in into a spot of high culture. This, of course, was a terrible idea which generated huge amounts of bafflement and yet produced some strange interludes. Joseph, for example was one of those who spotted someone he knew and stepped in to say hello. He turned and nodded at me:

'Scuse me teacher.'

'No problem.'

And I waited. He had the door shut behind him, leaning on it. He was a biggish guy in his thirties, long straight hair, starting to go a bit bald.

'What do you do in here then?'

'Shakespeare,' Ahmed said.

'Oh,' he said.

'Sit down if you like.'

'No, you're alright.'

'Well, sit down or fuck off,' Ahmed told him, so he sat.

He stayed with us for the rest of the morning and then, the next week, he had his name on the register and there he was. He never said much, didn't even look much at the book. When he did join in he'd generally got the wrong end of the stick and Matt would take the mickey, make gorilla faces and say things like, 'Fuckin durrr,' and twiddle his finger. Eventually he got a bit of a hard look from Joseph and he stopped it. Which surprised me because Matt was not at all given to being intimidated. Joseph, though, had something like the same effect that Maurice had had. Everything, when he was in the room, was just a bit quieter. From time-to-time he gave up all pretence and came along with his newspaper and spread it on the desk and went through it carefully, leafing it over page-by-page for the three hours we were there. I think, although I never broached this with anyone, that he just liked to be present when we were being clever. He was never going to be a scholar but he liked the thought that a bit of scholarship was going on and that he could say, back on the wing, 'I'm going to Literature this morning; we're doing Shakespeare.'

'What you?'

'Yeah, fuckin me.'

Or something like that. A lot of the guys liked to say things such as: 'There are a lot of intelligent men in this prison. You'd be surprised.' They used to say it to me all the time when they were training me. These days I get in first and say it to them to make sure that they know what they are. There is enormous respect for learning and intelligence, for culture. Not for showing off though. It's the same sort of respect that exists for politeness and cleanliness, for not being what the guys call 'ignorant.' It is important to dispel the myth that prison is the place where we put the demons. It's not an easy place, but it's not as simple as that.

Joseph palled up with Ginge and they became something of a double act. They inherited a budgie and called him Budgie Blue Legs.

'What you call him that for?'

'He's got blue legs.'

'Oh.'

Ginge thought that they could train him as a killer budgie but he was too good natured so they tried to teach him to make obscene remarks about the officers. Budgie Blue Legs never really mastered Brummie and as they'd inherited him from a Jamaican his speech patterns became a bit garbled. Sometimes they brought him to class. They would put him into the cardboard tube from a toilet roll, just his little beaky head poking out, one of them would have him in the top pocket of his shirt.

One day Joseph told us his story. I don't know why he went into it. We were doing *Macbeth*, so that might have sparked him off.

'I've got nine years Al.'

'Blimey, that sounds a lot.'

'For defending my daughters.'

'How do you work that out?'

Joseph was dead serious. 'This feller was shooting his air rifle at people. Leaning out of his bedroom window. Know what I mean?'

I nodded.

'Taking pot shots at people. So, I went over and I told him to stop it. I wasn't nasty about it, not at all. But he reared up and started telling me he was gonna shoot my girls. Telling me to fuck off. All that. He really upset me. I went home and, well, I started brooding about it.'

Joseph looked down at the desk then around the room. There wasn't a sound. We had an idea of what was coming.

'Next morning I got my machete and I went over there. I swear I wasn't going to do anything, just scare him so he'd stop shooting people. He was an idiot and he went off his head, started threatening me. He was gonna do this and that. And, he was really abusive. So I chopped him up. Nine years, for defending my daughters. It's not right.'

'It's not,' I said and I meant it.

'And the trial, the trial it was ridiculous. The only evidence given against me was by the geezer I'd chopped up. What did he know, he had fuckin' brain damage. It'd taken them six months just to teach him to say yes and no. He was a terrible witness. But, I got nine years.' We were all bursting with laughter and trying not to. Joseph was absolutely serious, the innocence and bewilderment of Bambi in his eyes.

One morning he was missing.

'Where's Joseph?' No-one knew. About eleven o'clock he came in.

'Just come to say goodbye.'

'What?'

'Yeah, I'm out this morning.'

'You never said.'

'Yeah well, don't like a fuss. You know what my wife and the girls have done? They've kept all my presents for me. You know, six years of Christmas and birthdays waiting for me to open them. Good eh? Tell you what though, you know how long I've done? Six years, six months and six days.' The rest of the class gave him a round of applause.

Ginge was a bit forlorn when he'd gone. He had Budgie Blue Legs to himself but it wasn't the same. A few months later when Ginge was released he took Budgie Blue Legs out with him and Joseph met them at the gate.

One Thursday afternoon we were reading *Songs of Innocence*. There had been some releases, some moves to other prisons and there were only four of us. The door opened:

'Wanna hear some music?' We had all been concentrating and we looked up, a little bit taken aback.

'What you doin?'

'William Blake,' said Jonathon.

'Oh yeah, he's good he is.' Usual bullshit, I thought. He stepped into the room and put a violin case on the table. 'You wanna hear some music or not?' There was one right answer. He opened the case, took out a yellow duster and put it on his shoulder and then the violin. There was a bit of listening and adjusting and then he played Mendelssohn's Violin Concerto. And he really did play it, not a botched job, a real spell-binding recital.

'Alright?' he said. He put the violin away and left. His 'Alright,' hadn't really been a question.

'Who was that?' I said.

'He's up on the Lifer Wing,' said Jonathon. 'Can be a bit of a pain, truth be told … Got to fuckin give it to him though, haven't you?'

Even though I was getting used to being surprised by the prison this really was quite something. Eric took to dropping in; sometimes he would play, sometimes not. Sometimes he would sit with us for ten minutes, even an hour and join in with the poetry and from time-to=time he would recite something that he had learnt by heart. He couldn't settle, though, not for the whole lesson. He would sit for a while, stand, lean on the window ledge, sit back down. Then I heard that he had gone off to Drama and I lost sight of him for a time.

The first months in the prison were sometimes a little confusing. I had always been easily induced into other people's ways of seeing things and I had quickly started to see things from the points of view of my students. I would go home and tell my wife about my Literature Class. She would have none of my nonsense.

'What about the victims then?'

I had to own up to not having given a thought to the victims. Like most teachers, well, like most teachers of my generation, I had simply dealt with the class in front of me and I had let myself live in that contact. This is what I still do and it's what has to be done in order to remain effective.

My students, though, were not youngsters they were men and I had discounted how thoroughly I would be drawn into their world. The Prison Service isn't silly when it has its courses on Prison Craft, when it warns us about being groomed by prisoners. Had I been operating in the prison at large then I would have been in real trouble. In Education I only ever saw a tiny percentage of the prison population and that percentage had in it a large proportion of intelligent, bookish men whose spirits were intact. The fact that someone as naïve as I had been had been given the space to learn how to conduct himself was an indicator of the decency of the men who came to my classes.

Her Majesty's Philosophers

.

6

A Sort of Insult

I'm not sure how it came about but one day I mentioned that I was not actually an English graduate.

'Oh really,' Jean said, 'What did you do then?'

There is still something in me that is a bit reserved about this. I only did it because it was the most obscure and useless thing on offer. When I was a kid in Sheffield in the 1950s and 1960s I lived in a heartland of common sense: what you needed was a good trade, security, your feet on the ground you needed to know what was what. It was a dull, deadening narrative that I hated. I went to a technical school and we studied engineering; there was a machine shop and a foundry, drawing offices. It left me utterly baffled and ham-fisted and I wanted no part of it. But, change was in the air and I was able to do A-Level English and then, when UCAS came around I applied for Philosophy.

Philosophy. It was a sort of insult. No-one, including me, had any idea what it was except that it seemed to be as far away from the foundry and the machine shop as it was possible to get. It was skyborn, head-in-the-clouds. It was useless and, as everyone pointed out, would get me nowhere. Good.

'You did philosophy did you?' Jean was saying now, eyes gleaming with the romance of it all. 'I've always thought that we should have a Philosophy course here in the prison.'

Of course it had only just occurred to her but Gwen and Helen were in the staff room egging her on. Gwen wanted to make sure that I would have some takers and so she went off and spent the next couple of weeks selecting and recruiting. She found most of these students up on D Wing. It was the obvious place to look. D Wing was a little bit more steady, quieter than the other residential parts of the prison. We called it the Lifer Wing but it was in fact for men whose sentences were longer than seven years.

Because the prison was a Category-C establishment we had lifers who were, notionally, in the final third of their sentences or at least of their tariff, the period that they must serve in prison for punishment or retribution. Life is life it really does mean that a man's natural life is the span of his sentence (I think that there is some fictive notion of 99 years). However, on sentence the judge will indicate a tariff, a period of time which must elapse before a prisoner may first apply for parole, for licensed freedom. If this licence is granted then the prisoner is allowed out of prison, but is free upon conditions and these vary with each licence granted. The prisoner is also susceptible to being re-incarcerated without any judicial process if the conditions of the licence are breached—is subject to what is known as recall.

Making progress towards release on licence dominates the consciousness of life sentence prisoners. It is a progress which is enabled by a process of detailed and continuing assessment. Lifers, in fact all prisoners but especially lifers, attend courses—assuming they are available (there has been criticism in modern times about under-provision, meaning that prisoners cannot progress anyway)—which relate to their offences and to their personal and psychological development. They are under ongoing review from psychologists and probation officers and from most prison staff with whom they come into contact.

The system is focussed on risk and safety and, as far as I can see, almost always achieves its aim of protecting the public. It errs, if it errs at all, on the side of caution. From the point of view of a man with a life sentence this can be frustrating and sometimes appear to be even malicious but as Les remarked: 'I thank God for a government that resisted those Fascist bastards who would have strung me up.' Les committed a single offence; he is now free, on licence, living, I have no doubt, an ordinary, decent life.

Philosophy in the prison was a bit of a leap in the dark.

'They'll love it,' Gwen kept on saying.

Gwen, after donkeys' years with these guys really did believe in their goodness. 'He just wants his mum really,' was a typical remark for her to make when some shaven-headed 18-stoner had shuffled off, pouting, after one of her bollockings. So I shuffled off, obedient myself, to get Philosophy launched on the sea of scepticism that I was sure awaited me.

The first group she produced for me was overwhelming. Ahmed was there, of course, but along with him he had brought Simon, Shayne and Bernard. They strolled in and, in their various ways, took me to pieces. They opened up a part of my life where I gave my class in the morning and then went to bed in the afternoon. Most of the guys were as unsure as me about what was going to happen. Philosophy: it did have a bit of a ring to it, especially doing it in prison; it sounded rather wise, stately, a touch superior.

It didn't take long for us to leave that kind of nonsense behind. Shayne, direct as ever, got us started, 'Come on then Al, what's it all about, Philosophy? How would you define it?' I was tempted to ask him, 'What do you mean, definition?' but some merciful instinct for self-preservation stopped me. They didn't want some clever undergraduate posturing, these guys wanted an answer they could get a grip on right here and now, so I told them a bit about Socratic method, that of the idiot child.

'You know,' I told them, 'when some daft kid keeps on asking, why? why?' Yes, they knew about that. 'Well, that's all that Philosophy is. Philosophers just ask why.'

There was a certain amount of storm to weather.

'Is that it then? Is that all there is to it?'

'Well yes,' I said, suddenly fearful that they would walk out on me and leave me to face Jean and Gwen with the ruin that I had made of their bright idea.

Time went by and I settled down with a regular group of men, mostly from D Wing. People came and went, though, as sentences ended and new guys were shipped in this meant that there were quite regular crises as philosophy virgins were seduced into our strange ways. Philosophy attracted men who had long sentences to serve and they brought into class the hard faced generosity that gets them through the years. They said things that frightened me to death.

Shayne on abortion: 'If we could turn back the years, Sim, wouldn't it be better, knowing as we do now that you were going to turn out to be a murdering nutcase who's been nothing but a drain on society, wouldn't aborting you have been a good idea?'

Dear God, I thought, head-in-hands, he's gone too far this time. I ought to have warned him about all the trouble that Socrates was landed in by

Philosophy. But these guys were neighbours on the wing. They smiled at each other. Sometimes, less often now, I got a bad time for being a weakling. It was usually to do with my problems with authority.

'For God's sake Al will you use your authority and sort these bastards out.'

'I have no authority, I repudiate it, I spit on authority.'

'Don't start all that shit,' Simon would tell me, knowing my game.

'Right,' said Shayne, brusquely, 'come on let's get on with this.'

'I'll read this next bit shall I?' said Simon. I would shrug and away we would go.

Shayne was a real asset; he just kept on asking the obvious questions that no-one else would ask for fear of looking stupid. He knows nothing. Or does he? Were his questions just a bit too good naturedly naïve? I promised myself to get someone to have a peak in his pad where I suspect there were walls full of Philosophy books.

'Hold on,' he said, playing the devious Yorkshire simpleton, 'what's metaphysics then?'

Before I could tumble into his trap Bernard turned to him and treated us all to a lucid, delightful explanation. Bernard was the youngest by far and got terrible stick, but I suspected that he had just done himself a power of good.

'Right, okay,' Shayne said nodding gently into Bernard's beaming face.

We had been talking about Aesthetics and I started to realise that Philosophy had the potential to create all kinds of perils. Aesthetics led us on to censorship and one week we had been reading J M Coetzee on taking offence. Coetzee suggests that taking offence is a transaction where the powerful and the powerless exchange roles and potencies. Far too late it dawned on me that making this explicit could get one or two of the more idealistic guys into trouble back on the wings where shifts in power, suspected or real, could have swift and devastating consequences.

'Now don't try this at home,' I kept on saying, panic mounting as I wished more and more that I had stuck to Epistemology or Philosophy of Mind. Fortunately I had Ahmed and Simon in the class. These were the steadiest men you could hope to meet, both well into their second decade of imprisonment. Men I admired. Both of them scholars who put me to shame. They tried out the idea, tried its fit into various contexts: Apartheid South Africa, Family, Prison. Shayne, who had really taken a shine to my version of Socratic method harried them into explanations, forced the occasional pursed lipped concession. They watched me struggle to get a word in and smiled as they saw my temper going and language deteriorating. I was so unpleasant in one session that I brought in a bag of sweets by way of apology. They were not impressed.

'He only bought these,' Ahmed pointed out, without a hint of a thank you, 'because he was such a right bastard last time.'

I hadn't met Simon before the Philosophy classes started. Before we could begin with Philosophy there were things he had to get straight. He started me off with some conventional politics, some remarks about New Labour and then we were into the history of the Labour Party, trades unions and their relationship with Marxism. Somehow we'd drifted into Darwin and scientific method before I realised that he was interviewing me. He was a slightly built blond haired guy and he sat there with his flask of tea in our shabby classroom wondering if he would award me a fellowship at the Oxbridge college he obviously ran.

Simon taught me how and when to go onto the attack. If I hadn't gone for him, he wouldn't have stayed in the class. This was quite a complicated interview. I not only had to know more than him but I also had to say up front when I didn't. But, not submissively. 'Well, I don't know anything about that, Simon, but what I do know is that your way of presenting that particular case is just not good enough, feeble-minded even. Just think will you, just for once in your life?' Mostly the teaching life is a life of restraint and understanding; with Simon there were wonderful moments when I could just let fly.

Ahmed would say: 'That's a bit harsh Al.'

And I would say: 'Well, fuck it,' and away we went.

Simon was absolutely determined to be himself and, to be honest, it could be a bit wearing. There would be heart stopping moments when, in a room where there were half a dozen drugs offenders, he would say,

'Anyone who deals smack is just a fucking scumbag and anyone who does smack is just a fucking moron.'

A quick look around at the faces, 'Alright?'

There was some bleak part of him that didn't care. I often found myself defending people against him or perhaps I was defending Simon from the reprisals, which, to me, looked likely. Someone, inevitably someone a lot bigger than Simon, might mention God.

'You fucking moron,' Simon would remark, venomously, 'only a fucking moron would believe in God.'

Or some similar opening gambit.

'That's a bit harsh Sim,' Ahmed would say which would prompt me into finding a way through the storm of emotion that Simon had generated.

'That you see is the sort of emotional response that first order distinctions can generate. When Simon explodes like that Philosophy wants to pull him back into something rather more cold-blooded.'

'Yeah,' Simon would say, 'fuckin right.'

And away we would go again.

We were a small group and mostly we institutionalised Simon's enthusiasm, although I sometimes felt anxious, even panic stricken, at the way things were going. It was difficult for newcomers but then quite often Simon himself took them in hand. There were close conversations during breaks or while I was doing the register.

'You can't come in here taking offence,' I heard him say. With Philosophy you have to leave your feelings at the door. It's special, alright, so just forget about your ego.' I glanced up and gave him a bit of a look. Cheeky bastard, I thought.

'Simon,' Shayne said, dead pan, 'is entirely without ego.'

I realised, too, that who was in the class was not entirely up to me. There was a certain amount of vetting and selecting going on up on the wings. When Steve first came to Philosophy he sat there, quietly taking us in. He had come down from the Lifer Wing with Jason and I suppose that the guys had auditioned, and then recruited him for the class. They were pretty choosy about who came into Philosophy and made short work of anyone who wasn't up to their high standards. It was nice of them, I think, to be as delicate as they were about my feelings, leaving intact, for me and for the management, the illusion that I was in charge. Out in the corridor at tea break I heard Steve telling his pal, 'Yeah, its Philosophy, man, we were talking about spider shit' (No, don't ask).

Simon grabbed him. 'Just keep your fucking trap shut about this, alright? Best kept secret in the prison, this class. We don't want the fuckin riff-raff coming in.' It was the most enormous compliment and I still cling to it. Even so he could be a bit trying.

'Why don't you come to Literature Simon?'

'What, all that made up old fashioned shit?'

'Why not? Why not have a telly in your cell?'

'What? I don't want their telly. They can stick it up their arse.'

Any hint of a search and he would take off all his clothes.

'I was brought up a nudist. I don't care do I?' He knew that the officers did, though, and that the rules prohibited nakedness even during a strip search. He liked a bit of innocent teasing.

'Always, when I have a piss test, I fill the bottle right up to the brim so that they spill it and make a pissy mess everywhere.'

After he went to his D Cat and had a little bit of freedom I heard that he had joined a debating society in the local town; apparently he was winning prizes. I imagined him tearing into people at the local Chamber of Commerce. Was he telling them to fuck off, calling them stupid bastards? Part of me hoped that he was, but another part of me knew that he was too shrewd to do that.

Simon's distrust of television was well placed. In-cell television when it was introduced meant that things changed. The culture of obsessive reading was badly dented and a new dimension of 'Did you see?' was added to lessons. Simon despised the whole thing as simply another means of control that a devious and insinuating regime was deploying. He thought, too, that all of it, all of television, was simply crap. Not that he thought either of these two things with all his mind but thinking them at all preserved some part of himself against what was being done to him.

For the first few weeks after in-cell TV we went through something of a cultural revolution; it was all 'Did you see' and East Enders and it would be difficult to exaggerate the impact of some of what came on later in the evening. Ahmed, came in one morning, giggling and telling me about a new phenomenon on the wing. 'It's amazing Al,' he said, 'all the toilets flush at the same time.'

'You what?' I asked him, innocently puzzled. And then the penny dropped and I had hysterics and tried for once to suppress my imagination.

All of this horrified Bernard who had been locked up since he was 17 and hadn't seen post 8.30 pm television for five years. 'It's all sex,' he told me, shaking his head, 'even the adverts. The world's gone mad. It has Al, hasn't it?' It had.

For a short while it was like being a schoolteacher again. There we were in the English Literature Class, a few weeks away from the AS-Level exams and they were watching Eurotrash and The Antiques Roadshow and coming into class all bleary-eyed from late night repeats of I Love Lucy. How do you manage a homework crisis in the nick? There I was playing hell with a couple of armed robbers when their essays were late or a GBH merchant who hadn't done the reading. But Lord Reith knew a thing or two when he saw television as being the great educator. When things settled down and the novelty was over it really came to be seen as a mark of feebleness to watch rubbish. I overheard Stan saying: 'I thought I'd be watching crap all the time, you know what I mean, but I watch the documentaries and all the history stuff.' There was a little bit of swagger in his voice.

'I watch Coronation Street,' Rory told him.

Stan's lip curled, 'That crap.'

Rory gave him the sad, blue eyes: 'My Mum watches it,' he said, 'so I watch it and I can think of her watching it with me.' That shut Stan up and uncurled his lip and I gave my nose a surreptitious blow.

But Stan was right about the way in which a lot of the guys had managed to edit out the nonsense. There was a sense of being a bit of an intellectual hard man if you watched the right things. Even so the telly had an odd sort of influence, much odder than the passionate, random reading did. What sort of an Education was someone getting who watched all the OU programming, jumped from Micro Biology to Renaissance Architecture to Advanced Statistical Analysis in the small hours and then tried to thread it all into my lesson on Phillip Larkin?

One of the officers shrugged and said to Bernard: 'Well, it's just one more thing that can be taken away from you isn't it? It sounded a bit cruel but in fact television had turned out to be a good tool for managing behaviour. Three 'strikes' or 'nickings' and it was quite possible to slip down to Basic Level which included no telly.

Television really was valued and so when there was a handful of staff running a wing of 60 or 70 men something that was both a sanction and a diversion was worth its weight in gold. More positively, television kept prisoners in touch with the texture of the outside world. The men who came to Education made me realise how much of Reith's intention to educate still survives. They find their way into Science, Politics, History and, in Rory's case, Opera. He was telling Stan about it.

'You like that sort of thing do you?' Stan asked him.

'Yeah I do actually and that woman, that soprano, she's got these really fantastic tits.'

7

A Certain Amount of Rivalry

Jenny taught Drama in the old industrial cleaning workshop. She had been teaching in the chapel but there had been some kind of contretemps with the vicar and someone, she thought it might have been a reprisal, had poured a cup of tea in the back of the telly. Some of the guys thought that she might have done it herself.

'You know how she can be,' said Neil.

I could see his point, but no, she wouldn't. I'm sure. Whatever the truth of the matter, the Drama Class had been exiled to the old workshops, a stark wilderness of fluorescent tubes, bare brick walls and thick metal mesh at high windows.

'All of this,' she said, 'will be painted. I want the guys to paint the scenery and so on directly onto the walls. There will be tiny tables and chairs around them, like a nightclub.'

And there will be. The last time she needed props she marched a group of cons over to the stores and asked the officers for beds and bedding. 'There was a certain amount of ribaldry,' she told me and I could imagine her narrow-eyed, patrician sneer. 'We're doing Bouncers this time, as you know. The lads do all the parts from thugs to tarts'

'How is it?' I asked.

'Worrying,' she said. 'Drop in and see.'

The guys came in like an avalanche, unlock had been a bit late and they dived in straightaway. There was a new bouncer in the cast, the original one was in Segregation for fighting.

'He was so good,' Jenny said. 'I went over to Seg to see if I could have him back, but they told me that they regularly saw another side of his personality than the one he revealed to me.'

Dave and Graham were taking Scott, the new bouncer, through the opening moments. I had never, anywhere, seen such a threatening, gleeful, abandoned, slant eyed, fear-inducing performance. Then, straight from terrorising me, they were into the slag-fest of the ladies hairdressers; same shaven headed cons, but they spanned into a world of third rate tarty backcombing that had a horrible thread of contempt running through it. When things went wrong Jenny stepped in sweetly, her quietest, poshest voice taking the venom out of the air. They towered over her, five foot two and genteel, and she gave them notes in a new, listen-to-me voice that cut. They listened.

Scott had never been in Drama before, the guys seemed to have auditioned him on the wing and pulled him in. 'They have such high standards,' Jenny told me. 'You can work on your lines Scott can't you?'

'Nothing else to do,' he said, 'I'm on Basic.'

'Try to be good,' she pleaded, 'we don't want to lose you.'

She got Scott to walk through his bit of the hairdressers.

'I'm not playing a woman,' he said, sticking his chest out.

Dave took him in his arms, 'Don't be like that darling.'

'Fuck off, don't touch me like that.'

But they'd got him on the back foot and he did it.

'I look a right cunt.'

He slapped his hand over his mouth, 'Oops, language, sorry.'

Jenny smiled.

'Jenny, what are you doing?' Dave said, 'we're all waiting'

'Helping Scott,'

'Well, go and sit down and then we get on with it.'

She smiled, curtsied, wiped the smile and glared.

'Dripping wiv talent I am mate,' said Dave.

Eric grabbed me, 'Come and look at this Al.' Jenny and I left the bouncers to it and went with him. She had another group doing A-Level Theatre Studies and Eric had made a video of their exam piece. We crammed up in the old stock cupboard to watch it.

'We're supposed to look little in this.'

'Little.'

'Like ghosts.'

'Meant to be devils.' They were whispering comments at me, pulling me in to their small group.

Jenny told me about them. 'When they first saw themselves on video they were a bit shamefaced. "Is everything we do aggressive?" they asked me, it was, really, a sad little moment. But they wore that out. Nobody lets anybody down and if you come in here you do what you say you'll do, no excuses. They're really picky about who they'll work with. Sods they are. There's a lot of rawness here and a lot of safety. People need to play and it has to be safe, safe for everybody. The safety of a role lets them explore things about themselves that they wouldn't dare to normally.'

She gave me a quick flash of her manic, green eyes. 'Not that I'm a therapist,' she said, coldly. And she isn't. She took no prisoners: she would lose her temper, rant and rave, explain, cajole, tell somebody off and then step back and wait. 'I kept them at it all day, yesterday. They ate on their feet. They were very tired at the end and I suppose that I should have praised them. I said it was quite good. I don't want amateurism.'

At the end of the afternoon I casually asked Dave and Graham what they'd been in. 'Johnny Bareback for Health and Safety; Guys and Dolls, Nathan Detroit I was. Bill Sykes in Scrooge. A barman, a bank robber, masques, poetry readings, youth and community work.' And they gave me the stare just in case I thought they weren't serious about all of this. Jenny and I watched them go back to the wings, 'Bless them,' she said.

A couple of weeks later I bumped into her and she gave me the bad news: one too many of her guys had been shipped out, one too many in solitary and she had had to abandon Bouncers.

'Doing a play, it's such a vulnerable thing in the nick,' and for once her chin is down.

'Can't you find some less difficult blokes?' I asked and got a scowl for my trouble.

She brightened up, 'We're doing a review, a cabaret, much less chancey.' She grabbed my arm. 'My friend,' she said, 'has a theatrical supplies business and she's let us have the most amazing things. The lads are going to need some bottle to do this in front of a prison audience I can tell you.' She shouted with laughter: 'Drag, drag? You've never seen anything like it. My God, you should see what they do with the feather boas.'

Then, Gwen came to Jenny with a much more sober proposal.

Abuse and neglect, abandonment, lovelessness and cruelty were the currency of childhood for many of the men. In the prison the parenting skills courses were always full of guys who wanted to get it right for their own kids; they didn't want to hand on the damage.

Safe Ground's 'Fathers Inside' is a two-week intensive experience which not only answers questions like, 'How do you run a children's party?' and 'How do you tell a story?' but confronts the men with the emotional maze of being a parent and being a child. Safe Ground nearly killed Gwen and Jenny. I thought that they seemed a bit subdued before the end-of-course presentation by the men.

'How's it gone then?' I asked them.

'It's been painful. For everybody,' Jenny said. 'The lads have been lovely though.'

'And they've been shits,' said Gwen.

Just before they were due to begin Jenny went and stood with them, trying to bring the panic down to a manageable level.

'I'll be a sight better when this is over,' Paul managed to tell her. It's not an audience I would have fancied: a selection from the Lifer Wing, some of the probation staff and a couple of managers from the further education college. And Number One Governor in the front row.

Paul began the narration, telling us about the visits room. 'This,' he said, 'is where children see their fathers.' The guys were on stage, a son and his mother come to see dad. The child's distress, mood swings, naive openness, the man's stumbling attempts to be somebody you can rely on, the doomed forcefulness. The child's face would break your heart. The guy who was playing the wife did it unbearably, a woman absolutely involved with her husband, strong and crumbling in an instant.

Then Paul, suddenly confident, let us off the hook and told us about writing and telling children's stories.

'I've never read to my kids. And I've got to.' Steven, Joe and Gerard step up and read us stories they have written: Biscuit Town, The Ransoming of T Rex, Norman's Forest. The gentleness of it froze us, sitting there behind razor wire and bars in that bleak room, listening to what the Sugar Monster did next.

Graham scared us to death. He was just about to begin his spot when his face came up full of anger. He batted a chair out of his way so that it spun from the stage. 'I've had enough of this,' and he was off on a tirade, 'and I'm sick of bloody Gwen. And you,' pointing at Jenny, 'whatever your bloody name is.' He rounded on Number One Governor and just as I was thinking, 'Oh shit, no don't do this,' he broke into a smile, a grin, a laugh. 'Had you going there didn't I?' he says. 'You bastard,' said Jenny.

Afterwards, when she had calmed down a little, she told me, 'There's a lot of truth in what Graham did, you know. There have been some difficult times this last couple of weeks.'

'It's opened some old wounds, this has,' Paul said.

'I didn't like it at all,' said one of the others. 'It was too intensive. I've really been worried about this.'

Joe came and stood with me and said, softly, into my ear, 'It's not just little kids who have to meet their parents in the visits room. I have to meet my mum and dad like that and I'm 32. Mum and dad are in their seventies—imagine how they feel.' That's what all of us had done, imagined the feelings of our mums and our kids.

Jenny and I began to think about university courses that might be open to the guys when they got out and I went to talk about this with Ian Spiby, who was Head of Drama at the university. Jenny had the external examiner coming in to see the drama practical and we wondered if Ian might like to come along as well. He thought it was a great idea. He wanted to take the chance to look at Dave who had just sent off his UCAS forms.

It was the end of January and I was standing with Ian in the middle of the prison yard. There was a storm of wind and dark rain shaking around us.

'Oh God,' he said looking upwards, 'look it's razor wire.' It is easy to forget what a daunting first impression prison can make. In his UCAS reference I had made Dave sound like Laurence Olivier and we wanted him to shine his way into a university place. It was an important afternoon for Dave and for his pal James: there was Ian from the university, the A-Level external examiner in to see their performance piece and, most worryingly of all, they had an audience. They didn't seem too bothered. 'Had to be Shakespeare didn't it Al?' Dave told me. 'Everything else is crap by comparison innit?'

'Jenny, this external examiner?'

'What about him, James?'

'His first time in a prison is it?

'So?'

'Could give him a bit of a scare couldn't we?'

'Don't you dare,' she grabbed a handful of his shirt, 'don't you fucking dare.'

Jenny sat with Ian and I in the audience and I could see that she was pretty wound up. 'All of them,' she said, 'all the cast, the others as well, they've worked really hard to get all this up and running for the A-level lads. I've been really glad of Derry,' she whispered, being discreet, 'perfect stage manager for this lot. He just swept in and sorted them out.'

'How?'

'Fear,' she said, smiling. 'Fear and threats. Wait till you see the King. They've made a golden throne specially.'

I wasn't ready for the impact that Dave would have on me. Only a few feet from the front row a ragged green elf, face full of light and, shamelessly improving Shakespeare, delivering his own introduction to a prison bound *Tempest.* Then he was all over the stage flitting like a malicious crab teasing with what he knows and the rest do not.

'This is all his idea,' Jenny told me, amazed like me at the sheer brazenness of the risk he was taking. This was after all a prison audience and his costume on its own, a tattered, emerald frock that gave off flashes of white sinewy flesh, was high wire without a safety-net. My heart was in my mouth. His wasn't: he crept, hid, implored, a crouching tattered sycophant on the make.

Thou didst promise to bate me a full year, applying wretchedly for parole to Prospero, captive himself. He slithered back, a *nymph o' the sea,* in a whirl of blue satin. The words snarled and wheedled their way from the back of his mouth, a malignant scouse Ariel who you'd set poisoned bait for if you thought he was in your back garden.

Foolishly, I couldn't help but resent the external examiner sitting in judgement; I hoped he knew what this had cost. It shouldn't make a difference, of course I knew that, but it damn well did. Jenny didn't show a flicker of concern, 'They're wonderful,' she turned and looked at me, 'of course they are,' and I had to scrape my heart off my sleeve.

James was Caliban. Stripped to his tattoos he dragged out a no-necked, bullet-headed, scab-knuckled savage. The rasp in his voice spilled up into his eyes, radiant with spite. His slack mouth slobbered up the booze from Gerard's gormlessly drunk Stephano and, mistaking a new master for liberty, he laid out for us the dreadful ironies of freedom and captivity.

It was a stunning play to see in a prison. Ian Spiby was stunned, 'Oh we'll have him,' he said and went off to speak with Dave who was out of costume now but still posing away in his make-up and hair, ready to give autographs.

'This is what they wanted,' Jenny told me. 'So risky. But then again they're risky people aren't they. No point in denying that. They'd never have got anywhere near this if we'd tiptoed around. Three weeks ago we lost Trinculo, shipped out, Danny just learned the lines, just like that and did it. Wasn't he good? I wanted them to be physical, use what they'd got and they bloody well did. What a morning though, what a morning. It was crap. James was sick in the dustbin. But you should see how they managed all of this back-stage. Stage craft you know, Stage craft.' She was a bit flushed and starting to gibber now as the relief got to her.

For me though it was Prospero's epilogue that lingered on. The big lad, Henry, offered the audience his hands, palms open, as if he were cuffed up, pleading, *Let me not dwell in this bare island… Gentle breath of yours my sails must fill.*

They filled a few sails of their own that afternoon.

.

8

The Confidence Trick

Both Jenny and I developed an obsession about exams. After Matt and the Death Dealer had made such a success of their A-Levels we just started to think that they could all do it and I'm afraid that we rather piled on the pressure. It was a bit too much and I think that it brought out the martinet in both of us. To be fair Jenny was already quite tyrannical but there was I, shy, self-effacing, suddenly confronting lifers and men with sentences for God knows what.

'Don't be so bloody silly … How can you be such a wimp?' I found myself saying. Eddy simply stopped coming to Education.

'Where's Eddy?' I asked Phillipa.

'Well, actually,' I could see that she was a bit embarrassed, 'he's staying on the wing, in his pad.' Phillipa was the gentlest soul and I could see her concern. It made it all much worse.

'He said that it was too much pressure, that you were doing his head in. I think he might be having a breakdown. Sort of.'

It was the same with Danny. He wrote me one excellent essay about Edward II and then banged himself up and sent his books back. Funnily enough I didn't feel a grain of sympathy or responsibility for either of them. What I felt was angry. How could they be so short-sighted, stupid, weak? All I wanted to say was: why don't you just fucking do it? And that's what I did say and, of course it got me nowhere at all. A month later when, I suppose, they thought the coast was clear, they drifted back. By then I had developed a speck of sense and settled for being delighted to see them. Which I was.

It should have been a good lesson in reality for me but because the exams had taken such a grip, often a farcical grip, on some of the other guys, Jenny and I were swept away with the triumphalism of the whole business. It was an up-and-down triumphalism where sometimes some of the guys actually failed. An outright fail at A-Level took a bit of digesting, especially when the people failing were obviously able and well read. We thought, in the end, that it was probably about time, the ability to organize time and to realise that it was passing. Perhaps imprisonment devalued and reconfigured time so that the three hours of an exam could flit away in an inadvertent daydream or an endless considering and reconsidering of this or that in the middle of a sentence. They might fail once but no one ever left without finally getting an A-Level. When Alistair failed he sat, astounded, staring at the results slip for a few seconds and then he said: 'All right then, I'll do it again in January.' It was pretty impressive and he swept up a couple of the others who had crashed with him. They did it all again, no problem at all.

But, of course it wasn't at all a case of 'no problem' for most of them it was a terrible effort of will. It was a situation which carried a real chance of failure, a real chance of having to face humiliation. A man living a life up on the wing who gets up in the morning for Education and walks down the corridor with books under his arm is making a statement and a claim.

'Where you goin?'

'Education.'

'Fuckin Education? What you doin there then? What? You? Advanced English? Fuckin joke.'

It left the guys with a lot to lose and they, naturally, made a joke of it in public and trembled in private.

It was January when they guys did their AS-Level Literature exam. I didn't like it; it was a rotten week. They were all sure that they'd failed.

'Don't get your hopes up Al,' Luke told me, 'I screwed it up.'

On the morning of the first exam I had been up on the wings just to make sure that they hadn't forgotten. Andy was banged up and the officer had to take me down the gloomy corridor to his door. He was asleep. 'I was having a really deeply dirty dream,' he said, accusingly.

'Go on then, tell it me,' I said, always ready to show an interest.

'Dream your own dreams,' he said. But he promised not to miss the exam in the afternoon. 'Does your wife wear stockings?'

'What?'

'I thought if I could have a stocking over me face, I'd feel a bit more confident, like going on the rob, yeah, all masked up.'

A few weeks later Helen, our posh secretary, rang me at home to tell me that they had all passed. 'Fucking brilliant,' she said, thrilled, and it struck me again how elocution lessons add a certain stylish radiance to swearing. That afternoon I smuggled in a chocolate cake.

We had a bit of a job deciding what books to do for the full blown A-Level. Wordsworth and Feminism came out tops. 'Colour Purple,' Rory insisted, 'and that Oranges book.'

'That's about lesbians isn't it?' Lesbianism is very popular in jail.

'Wish I was a lesbian,' said Rory, wistfully.

Even though he passed his exams Andy still has a credibility problem. 'When I came into prison, when I was a kid, I used to run around on the wing selling drugs and phone cards, talking to the right people, being a prick. I don't do any of that now'

Rory pulled a daft face at him. 'Go on then Andy, tell him,' nodding at me, 'what you do every night between six and eight.'

'I study.'

'You're a swot.'

'No I'm not.'

'Yes you are,'

'I'm not.'

'You are.

'I'm not.'

I sat there listening to this and I thought: these are the criminals that all the politicians are so anxious to be hard on.

'You,' said Andy, 'you want to turn that telly off.'

'I can't.'

'Course you can you soft gett. Anyway it's all right for you, I have to read things stacks of times before I can understand what's going on.'

'Oh yeah what about all those essays you wrote?'

'I only wrote them to see what was wrong with them.'

'You lying rat.'

'Everybody says I'm a liar, all my family say it. I was telling my mother on the phone about doing these two A-Levels, she says: "Andrew, you're lying again. You're not taking drugs again are you Andrew?"' He has us laughing at the posh scouse voice he gives his mother.

'My dad,' said Rory, 'he loves it. He sees this as a blip, me coming in prison. Coming to Education's the only positive thing you can show your family after you've screwed up. You feel like a kid talking about your exams over the phone. When I pass something they send me postal orders, you know, and cards.' Rory had just passed his certificate 9281 so that he could teach Basic Skills. Somebody told him that he couldn't do it, that he was a con. But he can, and does. He had listened to me talking to Andy about his terrible handwriting. I was worried that not being legible might damage his chances in the exam. Andy was taking quite a bit of convincing. His approach was that it would probably be alright and we could hope for the best. Rory said: 'Write me something.'

'What?'

'Go on write me something.' We all stared hard at Andy and so he wrote his name.

'You're holding your pen wrong.'

'How do you know.'

'I've got 9281.'

'What's that?

'It's my certificate, did it with Sue. It's so I can help dorks like you to do the sorts of things they should have done when they were five.' He showed him how to hold his pen. 'Go on try it now.' It was stunning; Andy's writing was transformed. It wasn't good but you could read it. 'Told you,' said Rory trying to be matter of fact. But he was as thrilled as the rest of us.

Ivan's problem, though, was that he just couldn't imagine himself ever doing anything successfully. He was sitting, staring at the desk, his head was down. 'I hate doing this, it's too much Boss. If you fail, how do you tell your parents that you've failed again?' This was Ivan's third attempt at his A-Levels; the last couple of times he was shipped out of the prison he was in just before the exam.

'It was my own fault,' he said and gave me a glum smile.

'This time then,' I told him. 'Even if you kicked off and got locked up in Segregation you could still do the exam. Might be ideal actually.'

His eyes widened with outrage, 'What do you mean, "might be ideal"?' It had entered his head that I might be planning to arrange a bit of solitary for him over the exam period and I could see that he was horrified. I hadn't thought of it before, but now that he had mentioned it… He did in fact make heavy weather of his second exam. He couldn't sit still, wanted a pee, needed a fag. Sue, who was invigilating, had to give him a rollicking, there were tears and then he got down to it and wrote the paper.

Steve, doing life, phoned his mum before the exam and again after to tell her how he had got on.

If this lot were the hardened toughs who are laying siege to society then they ought to have been tougher than this. Charles couldn't sleep; Luke needed reassurance after every intelligent, lucid paragraph that he wrote; Rory couldn't do it, he couldn't, he really couldn't.

Never again, I was thinking to myself and then Lee, who had just arrived, said, 'I could do this exam couldn't I? I've got plenty of time you know.'

9

Fluffy Blue Cup and Kenneth's Cock

Philosophy was and is an odd business. I had, in fact, always experienced it as an odd business. No-one in my family ever had any idea of what I was doing and there was always that question of, 'Where will it get you?' lurking around. In prison there was a tendency for Philosophy to find a place with conspiracy theorists and hippies and guys who really thought that drugs would expand their minds into truths and visions. It surprised me how tenacious a grip the 1960s had. It reminded me at times of that rambling flat we had on Micklegate when I was a student and I couldn't resist the odd anecdote. 'What you?' they said, incredulous. Then I went into my anti-drugs rant and they knew where they were again.

The best, or at least the most naturally susceptible, students were often the guys who were quite serious offenders, men doing sentences for violence, armed robbery or murder; those who had started off on long sentences with little or no schooling, who in many cases started coming to Education simply to pass the time. They could be a bit direct. Karl, after about half an hour, said:

'What good is all this Philosophy crap?'

Not a bad question.

'You never get anywhere, do you?'

There were smiles all round and I could see them thinking, 'Go on Al, get out of that then.' They saw it in the way that they might have seen a fight, curious, impartial, not too bothered about fair play. The problem for me was, and still is, not to have a row. Simon could always get away with a spot of vicious denunciation but I was the teacher and, really, I had to cling on to respectability. Some quiet, reasoned argument was what was needed, and guile. How do you convince anyone that Philosophy is not a load of useless crap? I can't even convince my wife. But, I didn't need answers; what I needed was delay. Philosophy might be crap but it is also seductive. If I can keep them coming back for a couple of weeks then they will never be free.

There is a routine bit of sophistry that usually did the trick.

'Nobody,' I told them, 'ever went to war about Ohm's Law or car maintenance or for any practical reason at all; people go to war about History and Politics and Religion. So you can see, can't you, how Philosophy is the most down to earth and urgently necessary subject?' Montaigne was a good ally here; all that talk about the thickness of his prick went down a treat.

Keeping people on board might have been the first obstacle, but the really big one was persuading them that an argument is not a row. Stan's blue cup became a standard provocation. People would greet him: 'Hello mate, how's your cup? Still blue is it?' His grip on things would not allow him to accept that in some circumstances, in the dark for example, his cup might not be blue. 'It's a blue cup,' he would point at it, bulgy-eyed and shout and bang his blue cup up and down on the desk by way of proof. Quite amusing in its way, not nearly so tedious as *The Illuminati*.

Have you heard of them? You would have if you had taught in a prison. Every few months someone arrives who has read the book. The book, there is only one, proved beyond any doubt that there is a world conspiracy of a secret elite aimed at enslaving us all. I somehow didn't have the heart simply to denounce the grotesque stupidity of it all, especially not to muscular zealots who came trailing histories of casual mayhem behind them. Sometimes, though, my self-respect managed to drive out fear and I heard myself becoming abusive about standards of proof. This cued in the sly comments about how scary I was.

'He's lovely when he's angry,' James remarked.

'Deep manly voice,' said Steve.

'You should do press-ups Boss,' Kenneth chipped in.

'Don't let it get you down Al,' said Ahmed, after all my careful arguments about scientific method, evidence, logic, inference had failed to discredit a couple of crackly tapes from Radio Free America.

'Prison's a breeding ground for any kind of crack-pot idea. I'll tell you, one nick I was in, all down one side of the landing got converted to Fundamental Christianity and all down the other side Satanism had a right firm hold. They talked about it through their windows, all night, after bang up, egging each other on. It was a right laugh; chanting and signs and spells coming right up against psalms and all that hands and face to heaven routine across the suicide net.

Common sense was just as much of a problem. It could be hard to swallow the idea that obviousness was problematic. Karl had only just joined us and he said, in all innocence, 'Course there's a God, look at the sky, the clouds, look, look at the flowers. I have to confess that my heart made a leap of agreement towards him. But I had done my cold-blooded work only too well and the others took him apart, pointing out that his words contained a particularly weak attempt at argument from analogy. Karl's reaction: contempt.

'You can't tell me that. You must be mad. Use your eyes.'

'Use your brain,' Simon retorted, summoning up his best sneer to date.

I managed to get them back onto Descartes' *Second Meditation*, but I could see trouble ahead when we got onto 'The Elusive I'. Some of these guys had several identities already, some struggled with handling just one. Sure enough we got into an intellectual rip-tide.

'It's not just your mind though is it? Even physically you change,' said Stan. 'In seven years time every cell in your body will have been replaced. You'll be completely different.'

'What everything?' Kenneth was stunned by this news.

'Yeah.'

'What, even my cock?'

'Yeah.'

What? Are you saying that every seven years I get a brand new cock?

'Yeah.'

'That's brilliant.'

God alone knows what he thought was going to happen to him.

Having Simon and Kenneth in the same class was always a bit of a game. Kenneth would maintain that he couldn't read and Simon, in his own cantankerous fashion, always went for him. Simon read a lot, mostly science, and this made him a dangerous opponent in the seminar jungle. Philosophy of mind and Epistemology were his favourite hunting grounds and I was his favourite prey. He would go off on intricate, high tension revelations about theoretical physics that I didn't understand. He liked to punctuate this learnedness with, 'Fuckin weird man,' 'Blow your fuckin mind man I'm telling you,' 'Folding fuckin universe, very strange shit,' and so on. A bit like Charlie Parker taking wing on a long hypnotic riff.

On the other hand Kenneth became the sort of philosophical holy simpleton who you really needed to watch out for.

'Whereof we cannot speak,' he told Simon, 'thereof we should remain silent.' I don't know what Wittgenstein would have made of Kenneth, who told me stories about his past that I chose not to believe, but Kenneth was well firmed up with Ludwig. He was delighted to know that reality is rooted in language and that all of Simon's science amounted simply to a way of talking about the world and I could see that he took a real pleasure in telling Simon this. But, he always found Philosophy a little bit strange, always felt a bit awkward, a bit out of place.

'My pals,' he said, 'they would, they'd just chin you if you said things like this. They'd think you were attacking them.' Kenneth found a whole new way of giving you a pasting.

When Simon took him to task for being (a) 'very tasty' and (b) a Christian, Kenneth let him have the first lines of the *Tractatus* and then told him that being a Christian in his world made him a better man than he otherwise would have been and that the world, whatever that might be, is all that is the case. Then before we could get on to what it might be to claim that something is the case an officer came in and took Simon off to an interview with Sentence Review. I took my chance and got us back to Brain Events and Mind Events.

Philosophy of Mind, it drove Stan nuts: 'Where do you think your mind is Stan?'

'You can't say things like that to me, I'm a schizophrenic.' We all fell about laughing and asked his advice on how we can be sure that other minds exist. 'You can't do this,' he said, giggling himself, 'it'll get me all jumbled up.'

'Well, I'm jumbled up,' I told him.

'Yeah, but you're paid to be jumbled up. This Mind shit been doing your head in for years hasn't it and you've just dropped it in on us. I know why they poisoned that little bastard Socrates. We were all happy till you asked these stupid questions.'

Simon got back from his interview, stony faced, it had given him a body blow. There were three other lifers in the group, all of them into their second decade, and Simon's non-result caught them all on the raw. Kenneth and I kept quiet and let them talk their way through this within their own abrasive solidarity.

Just before we got going again Kenneth said to me, softly so that they couldn't hear, 'Listening to these guys Al, I couldn't do life, I couldn't.'

'If you get caught again they might life you off Kev.'

'I know,' he said, very quietly, 'I know.'

It was an achievement that Jean had been able to get Philosophy running in the prison and that her successor, Sue, has kept it going for nearly 14 years now is amazing. We don't call it Philosophy anymore, at least not on the mountains of forms that I am asked to fill in, and don't, every week, we call it Advanced Thinking Skills. Not a lie and yet it gives the impression that I might be doing something psychological, something therapeutic. I might well be. Our managers refer to Philosophy and to a whole range of other subjects as fluffy. Anything beyond Literacy and Numeracy: Fluffy. Fluffy or not we, at one time, had pushed out the boundaries of the department and there were courses in Literature, Sociology, Creative Writing, Art, Pottery, French, Spanish. As we got better at it we began to have waiting lists and the classes became too big to be altogether manageable or, in fact, safe. Classes where there was a chance, a certainty, of disputes occurring needed to be well-managed.

What I learned to do, especially in Philosophy, was to institutionalise conflicting viewpoints into schools of thought. Take for example a dispute about the reasons for such a large number of black guys in prison. Someone might well offer an explanation in terms of social control and that might provoke quite bitter comments about racism that could quickly evolve into a row. Showing how this could be stated from a Marxist or a Liberal or an Anarchist point of view had the effect of turning a row into a problem. It also opened up the way to pointing out how they were linking themselves to long lines of intellectual history. The great thing was to see how men who saw for example racism in a particular way were consistent in bringing the same intellectual framework to notions of, say, justice or censorship.

Groups of the guys would often fall into factions and so instead of a row I could ask people to put not their view but the Anarchist view. I could say things like: 'The McAllisterite view of this is ... and link Patrick's right

71

wing, liberal individualism with nationalism or Friedmanite capitalism. As the weeks went by people of similar views drifted into the Marxist corner or the John Locke enclave; they actually did start to sit together and have little sub-plots going on. This half-serious half-playful faction forming put an objective, ironic distance between the men and the views they held. We all had more space and could avoid investing too much ego and status in the business of winning an argument.

Philosophers are always supposing things, making up examples from real life to illustrate their abstractions. My teachers at university were prone to examples about railways, football, vases on tables, this book I am reading, works of art. Adultery was their particular favourite. A few years of teaching Philosophy in the prison made me wary of dragging in reality. I go to enormous pains to extinguish all remarks that begin with: 'What, you mean like when…?' because by now I have a rough idea of the chasms that await me.

We were talking about brain and mind. I think it was Simon who was claiming, quite reasonably, I thought, 'If you lose part of your brain you might well lose part of your mind,' when Frank stopped him. 'I've lost loads of my brain.'

'What?' We were spellbound.

'Yeah I was doing a drugs deal with some very dodgy terrorist guys. It'd all gone sour, God knows why and they shot me.' He pointed to the back of his head. 'Here, see?' We certainly did. In fact we all left our seats to have a good look and tap his metal plate. 'It went in like that, hit the corner of my jaw bone, ricocheted up, took out a load of brain, and out the top. Had to learn everything again, walk, talk, everything. But, I've still got my mind.'

'Ah,' said Ahmed, 'but is it still the same one?' It was a cruel thing to say and we all saw the confusion on Frank's face and laughed. It was a proper, thought-provoking example, not some mealy mouthed claptrap about what's on the table.

There is something, I think, about imprisonment that makes Philosophy a closely felt experience. No shortage of examples about justice, truth-telling, keeping one's word. The consequences of failing in these areas are much more devastating for my students than for most philosophers. Not keeping faith with your wife is one thing, not keeping faith with a Yardie quite another. For Kenneth it was Machiavelli who made the greatest impact. His face was alight, 'The Government,' he said, 'they're just another little firm aren't they? That's terrible. I should have read all this years ago, I'd have been massive, I'm telling you.'

It was Kenneth, again, who was impressed to find his roots as an Anarchist. Simon had been banging on, raving even, about the notion of the individual as a rational being free of all restraints of structure and hierarchy. Kenneth slapped the table, 'Yeah man we were like that when I was a football hooligan.'

'Oh no, Kenneth, you didn't do all that, did you?'

'I loved it,' he said, refusing to countenance my startled prissiness, 'I did. It was just like this anarchist stuff. I'm telling you. Some firms have got top lads. They even have different T-shirts, like an army, guys telling you what to do like they were officers. We didn't do none of that right? Everybody was equal, we'd get together and plot everything up. Get people to chase us, yeah, and then all turn together and give it to 'em. Gas. Knife.' Lost for a moment in the memory, showing us, left hand, right hand.

'Kenneth, you didn't.'

He gave me the big grin, 'Yeah we did,' and pulled up his T-shirt to show the scatter of stab marks.

'We were like brothers man.'

He stopped himself as though something were dawning.

'We loved each other. We did.'

Kenneth's examples really did put flesh on the cold, philosophical bone.

There was a brief spell when I had Charles, Ahmed and Simon in the Philosophy Class at the same time and the mornings rolled away with hardly a hint of the time passing. This was a delight; lessons which lasted for three hours could turn into a long hard slog where enthusiasm and invention died. If there was only one major voice, mine, then everyone, including me, could have more than enough of it. Classes were run in three hour blocks because we had to fit into the security regime of the prison. The whereabouts of everyone, at all times of the day, had to be known and if the count across the whole establishment didn't tally then everyone had to return to their cell so that a formal and accurate roll could be taken.

At 8.45 am the officers would collect my register, count the heads and lock us in. We might manage a toilet break at 10.15, but, essentially, we were stuck with each other until 11.45. Then the men would go back to the wings to eat, bang up until 2.15 and after that the afternoon in work or education.

Some men contrived to be really busy: they came to education, they had a job as a cleaner or in the laundry or they were an orderly somewhere, they went to gym or to the chapel or they were Listeners. It was possible to live a demanding and busy life in prison. Most men didn't. The men in Education tended to be intelligent, motivated and drug-free but elsewhere there could be inertia, resentment, anger, a lot of empty, decaying nothing. The prison staff were, quite rightly, intent on getting men into what they called purposeful activity. But, if the horse won't drink, it won't. It was the men who were most active who were least damaged by prison.

Simon, Ahmed and Charles were all lifers. Simon and Charles were into their second decades of confinement, Ahmed well into his third. His third. All three were witty intelligent men in whom I had complete trust and they never let me down. This was one of the bonuses of not being a real part of the prison. People who are in prison all the time, staff and prisoners tend to be cynical and suspicious, how could they not be? But, I taught at the university, went home to my wife and kids and the ordinary life of friends and shops and trees and flowers. I was absolutely determined to bring as much as possible of this into my classes. My ordinariness was their ordinariness.

Just be straight with people, I thought, and expect them to be straight with you. What if they're not, I thought ? So what? Just allow yourself to be deceived, it doesn't matter. And, so, from time-to-time I would say something like: 'I don't care if you are making a fool of me, telling me any old bollocks, fuck you, I can still be me and if you are being devious, well, I'd rather be me than you.'

Then Ahmed left. Ahmed's offence had a political dimension to it and the tariff on his life sentence had long been left behind. The decades of incarceration had not made him hard, not quite, but there was something matter of fact about him. He was a man who made few judgements about people and only responded to what was immediate. He had stories about all sorts of people, people he had met in high-security prisons who had done all sorts of things. Ahmed was only concerned to tell me if they could cook a good meal when all they had was an electric kettle, whether they were generous, brave, discreet, funny, intelligent. It was enormously liberating and taught me how to slip into moral neutral. I had not realised how sick and tired I had become of having to have an attitude, an opinion, about everything, how oppressive the hectoring of the media, the politicians, the moralists had become.

Someone brought up the Bulger case. 'They're children,' Ahmed said when an outraged Tory convict had been howling for blood.

'What you gonna say to that little kid's mother?'

'There's nothing anybody can say is there?' Ahmed told him. I think that he had got used to living in the middle of unresolved contradictions, a place where you only faced what was in front of you.

Ahmed was sent north to an open prison, a Cat-D and I didn't hear of him again until I was reading Jeffrey Archer's *Prison Diaries*. There he was, sticking up for Archer in some prison confrontation. It made me smile to think of the whole world queuing up to kick Archer when he was down and Ahmed finding the heart to behave decently. It made me think well of Archer too for giving Ahmed a bit of a boost in his book. At least it made me ashamed to join the mob.

A few years later, after we had signed up for the European Declaration of Human Rights and it really was impossible not to, Ahmed was released on licence. Twenty-seven years inside and now he's living a quiet, academic, life. Yes, I know, what do you say to the victim's family? There's nothing you can say, is there?

Her Majesty's Philosophers

10

It Can Get Quite Heated

One of the officers put her head around the door. She was a good looking young woman in her thirties, blonde, elfin. Her eyes lit up, 'Ooh hello sir.' There was something about her and then, yes, of course. My eyes lit up; it was Kelly. I remembered her straightaway. She had been in my sixth form class years ago when I was a schoolteacher and now here she was keeping order in the jail and looking out for me.

'Time for the lads to get back to the wing,' she said and then raised her eyebrows at the furious, finger-wagging row that was going on in my room. I shrugged.

'What can I do?'

And she said, 'Nothing changes does it?'

We had had a complicated morning, talking about Art. I thought that Art might have been a bit restful after the last few weeks of politics but things were worse, much worse.

This was Chris's first time in Philosophy and I had set out to protect him from the onslaught. I need not have bothered. Once we got on to Clive Bell and Significant Form he launched into a bitter denunciation of 'those Bloomsbury bastards.' Which I thought was pretty impressive not only because he knew what he was talking about but because it was so keenly felt. It let me get started on what the Marxist view might be, which provoked a bit of snarling from Patrick and Tom but brought Wesley in on my side, thank God. But then, I alienated Wesley by hinting that Surrealism was only fit for adolescent Fascists and he got out his Salvador Dali calendar and I suggested that we might burn it and that apparently was the sort of elitism that Chris really did despise in Clive Bell and then I lost my temper.

Losing your temper is one of those wonderful luxuries that we take for granted. You can just let yourself go and fall heedlessly into the moment. I found that I was doing it more and more. No-one minded; in fact, they all laughed. Alan going off on one and then slinking back feeling a fool, very amusing.

Towards the end of the morning I won back some credibility by introducing the notion that claims made about Art are first and foremost linguistic acts and I took refuge in the calm that was generated by the careful technical arguments. It didn't last. Patrick thought that, yes, a word that refers to everything can have a meaning and Wesley thought that, no, it can't. Mere words could not contain Wesley's new belief in Sausure and language as a system of differences and he was on his feet, impassioned, theatrical, until he saw us all smiling and making faces at each other. He put his hands up, sat down, 'All right, all right. Bastards.' Which let Patrick back in and Wesley was big eyed with the injustice of it all, back on his feet. When I got rid of them I had to lean on the filing cabinet and do a bit of Yoga breathing to calm down.

In the prison there were security issues that I didn't need to consider at the university. What had the greatest impact on me was that the officers needed to know where people were and this meant that the class stayed together for almost three hours. It was too much. I always tried to have a bit of a break but they just carried on

Every Friday it was the same. I had to go home and have a short sleep in the afternoon. Wesley assured me that, back on the wing, they carried on with this all weekend.

'You don't realise. It can get quite heated.'

Could Philosophy get the blame for the next major prison riot: Empiricist mob burns down D Wing, Aestheticians take Governor hostage, food revolt by Epicureans? I supposed that it would provide some sort of an answer for the people who kept on asking me what Philosophy is for.

My method, in Philosophy, was quite simple. I began with Plato and worked my way through to the 20th-century, dropping in on the philosophers I happen to be familiar with. My core text was Warburton's *Philosophy: The Classics.* This I would recommend to anyone setting out on a Philosophy course. I think that it would be quite possible to do an entire degree with no other books whatsoever. Why read Kant, for example, when Warburton has done it for you and got it down to just a few, entertaining pages. You might do it out of duty I suppose. This is not so unprincipled as it might sound. Well, it might be.

Quite often we read a couple of sentences of Warburton and that would be sufficient to keep us busy and entertained for a whole morning. Of course I had done a degree in Philosophy and so I was able to expand on the core text and sometimes I surprised myself at what I knew (and remembered knowing). If I uttered this kind of sentence in class then we might be good for a fortnight. The class simply rolled on in this way and I found myself beginning again with Plato every 18 months or so.

Men came and went and they dropped into Philosophy at whatever point we happened to be. Some men have been through the cycle two or three times, sometimes on the same sentence, sometimes when they came back after recall or reconviction. It was always nice to see each other again and I now have a small resource of men who can step up and take those parts of the course that they have done before. This is good for their morale and status and is a great help to my usually unsuccessful campaign to shed authority and responsibility. It is still difficult to work out who and what I am in the prison.

It all became much more confusing when I got a real job with a proper contract at the University of Northampton.

'How's the new job going?' Wesley asked.

'It's a bit weird Wesley,' I told him. 'Thursdays are driving me nuts.'

I began my working week in my new office in a new university and it was smart and busy and crammed with enthusiasm. From the car park I had to walk through the Fashion Department and it overflowed. The corridor was full of frocks and fabrics, great billows of colour and when I sneaked a look in the rooms there were tailors dummies, vivid upholstery, cloth, lace, pictures, tissue paper plans. There was the Drama Department and Fine Art. Every loonie in the university under the same roof. There were the girls who used to intimidate me when I was a kid.

'But I'm just an old buffer now,' I told Wesley, 'so I've got the confidence that being harmless gives you.'

Wesley gave me the cynical smile the little shake of the head. 'Yeah yeah, you say that.'

The university was like the prison really. I suppose that there were different tactics for self-protection but slipping into the role of harmless old buffer worked in both contexts.

'I'm not really an academic at all,' I liked to say to my students and to my colleagues, 'they've only got me in to do a bit of writing with you. Just a bit of a hack really.' So that the scraps of scholarship I did have shone out and gave an impression of endearing, false modesty.

And then, there I was, in the prison. From the safety of my physical decrepitude and harmlessness, I could pick quarrels with people who could make mincemeat of me, great big corridor fillers half my age. I found myself shouting at them sometimes. It was Philosophy of Mind and I was losing my temper about Dualism.

'Where is it then, where is it?' Why was I sneering at Spud, he'd only suggested that he thought that he might have a mind?

'Tucked up behind your left fucking ear I suppose?' Harmless.

No matter what we did to the Education Department, posters, art work on the walls, it still managed to be prison. The starkness shone through and with the Fashion corridor buzzing in my head it could be a bit too much. It was an unnerving business going back and forth between the university and the prison and it was easy to get confused. The students were drunken and feckless; the prisoners quiet and studious.

11

Was This Happiness?

Sometimes we found islands of calm. Sometimes there could be an atmosphere of seriousness and I would slip into thinking that all of the prison was like it was in our Philosophy Class.

We had been talking about social contract theory and how Hobbes and then Locke made use of the notion of nature.

'Of course,' I said, 'they never thought that there had ever been such a thing as a state of nature.' And as this was pretty standard stuff I got quickly into my university stride: lecturing, explaining. But, the State of Nature had been ringing a few bells.

Chris interrupted. 'When we have chips,' he said, 'they often have to get one of the screws to the servery to serve them.'

'Yeah,' said Phil, 'chips can cause serious problems.'

'People competing for scarce resources,' said Chris, 'you get in a chip contest and life can be nasty, brutish and short.'

'Yeah,' said Phil.

'It can't be like that all the time,' I said, hoping for the best. I could see, though, how chips could spark things off.

'Not like that Hobbes,' said Phil, waving his hand, searching for the name. 'Like that other feller.'

'Locke,' said Nick, giving him a prompt.

'Yeah,' said Phil, 'him.'

'Let me tell you a story,' said Chris and we settled back because Chris liked to tell a story and he was usually pretty good.

'One place I was in we had a nice, peaceful wing. True, there were all sorts of things going on: Londoners against Northerners, Africans against Jamaicans, Chelsea against Man U, all the usual, but nothing nasty. It was nice. And then this Ogre was moved onto the wing and he decided that he was going to take over. This one guy he protested and he was beaten, he was cut. Terrible, terrible. And you know what? All the people who'd been opposed to each other they was shaking hands and agreeing something had to be done.'

'Social Contract,' I said.

'No,' said Ben, 'Laws of Nature.'

And we were away: did the guys have the right, the natural right, to set fire to the Ogre's cell?

'Yeah,' said Phil.

'They fuckin' did it anyway,' said Joel.

'And,' said Chris, 'the best thing was that this kid, just a kid, early twenties, he went up to this big Ogre and he was a big, big guy, Al, and he says to him, "The person you hurt was very well-respected and you thought that you could do that without any consequences but there have been consequences and there will be consequences." I was really moved by him. He was only a kid. And he spoke nicely, not rough. Anyway they had to shift the Ogre off the wing.'

'Hobbes's first Law of Nature,' I told them, trying to find some kind of a moral message, 'seek peace wherever possible.'

'Well we did,' says Chris.

'And they enforced the Law of Nature,' says Carl, 'which is their Natural Right.'

'You've been reading again,' I said and he smiled.

'I would think,' I said, and I was feeling my way a bit, 'that if you're two'd up, then each cell is like a tiny commonwealth and I'll bet that some are more successful than others.'

'Yeah,' said Phil, 'you're not kiddin.'

'When I came into prison,' said Joel, 'I was terrified. I was. I was thinking, "There gonna rape me; I'm gonna get raped." I was two'd up with this guy and I'm thinkin, "I'm gonna go to sleep and he's gonna stab me."'

The guys were all laughing; the way you laugh when you recognise something.

'I was more than two years in that cell with that same guy. He looked after me; we shared everything.'

He makes a gesture with both hands as if he were breaking something into two parts. 'He's my fuckin' brother. Always.'

It was the sort of remark that made me think about imprisonment: two years in a small cell, two'd up and two years these days is not such a long sentence. It made me think about Dean and his notion that every man should do a prison sentence.

'You really find out who you are.'

It made me realise that Philosophy and Education generally were only a tiny island in the dreadfulness of prison.

Whenever I went into the prison, through Reception, the locks would click and buzz and let me through. I would pick up my keys and unlock the first of several security gates. Then there were the fences and the wire and the tight rows of windows and the noise. In Philosophy, we were going to talk about Bentham and Mill. About happiness. About pleasure. When I thought about it I was a little bit afraid that the guys might think I was winding them up.

On the way in, I passed Terry, looking even glummer than yesterday, standing there with all that weight on him, smoking a roll-up. He was looking at it scornfully, as if he didn't want it at all.

'You all right, Terry?'

'Yeah,' he said, 'I'm doing all right.'

He tried out a smile. When I got to my classroom, Walter was already there, waiting. He was doing life. Well into his sixties now, he had just a few scraps of grey hair left on the pink of his scalp. When Oliver came in, Walter started a fight. Not a real fight, of course. This was a fight that lifted your heart. Walter, in his trainers and his roll-bottom jeans and the prison blue-striped shirt, was dancing in under Oliver's guard and giving him a one-two in the ribs, laughing all over his face, one-two-ing him again. Oliver was cracking up and flicking a couple of slow ones at Walter's head, just touching him. Oliver is six-six, so Walter had to reach up to whack his ribs. Big fists darted all round Walter's head. Laughing, both of them. Was this happiness? They were doing better than I would have done.

For someone like Rory, doing his first sentence, prison was not a smiling matter at all. As the months went by he was changing in front of my eyes. He couldn't stop talking, telling stories, laying down the law, so that Luke had to say,

'Shut up.'

'Doing it again, am I?'

'Yeah, just button it for five minutes. Give us a break.' It sounded a bit rough but he knew that Luke was watching out for him

Darren was growing paler every week. And Tim, from time-to-time, vanished behind his door. It doesn't suit everyone, prison.

Of course, they thought that Bentham's pleasure calculus was a strange notion and, of course, it is, all that weighing up of the higher pleasures against the low.

'Is this a higher pleasure, then?' Richard asked.

'Is what a higher pleasure?' said John.

'This. Us doing this. Philosophy.'

'Well, I think it is,' I told him. 'What would you rather be doing?'

It was a silly question and off we went with a long list of blondes and spliffs and a large scotch and an afternoon in bed with the Cheeky Girls. Spud stopped them with the dreadful idea that it might be possible to be happy in prison.

'I suppose I am, you know, contented. I keep to myself, get on with my studying. I've got all my life in a few footsteps. I go from my pad to the servery, my pad to the gym, my pad to Education. I was lying on my bed and thinking, no, this can't be right. I can't be happy in prison. That's wrong.'

'I know what you mean,' said Luke. 'You just get used to the life, and then you panic because it's not a life you should get used to.'

'The Utilitarians might think you'd cracked it,' I suggested.

Then David put his head round the door.

'Do you want to see what I've done?'

'What have you done?'

'I've made this lamp.' It's in the shape of a thatched cottage. 'I reckon it's brilliant. I'm gonna give it to my mum.' He stepped into the room, held up the lamp and beamed.

'Where'd you do that, then?'

'In the pottery. Pottery Sue showed me how to do it. Fired it, glazed it, everything.'

'Are you happy about doing it?' Spud asked, and it went quiet.

David looked a bit worried at the way the whole room was hanging on his answer.

'Yeah,' he said, 'course I am.'

'And would you,' said Spud — and you could have cut the tension with a knife — 'swap the lamp and the way you feel about it for a nice blonde and a pint of lager in the pub?'

David looked puzzled. 'What are you asking me that for?'

'Would you?' said Robert.

David thought about it. He shook his head.

'No, no of course not.'

These sorts of sensitivities were not unusual but they persisted in seeming unusual because of the place we were in. When the same men who described, in matter of fact voices, lives of dislocation, violence and cruelty, produced intelligent and sensitive responses to a world of ideas the effect on someone like me was troubling. I realised quite early on that some of the chaps would worry and brood about things. Robert was normally the most feet on the ground person you could imagine but in the middle of one class he stopped as if something had struck him, suddenly, out of the blue.

'Alan?'

'What? What's the matter.'

'You don't reckon I'm going to Hell do you?'

'Why should you?'

He was in prison but even so he wasn't a bad bloke .

'I went up to the chapel the other night. I got it wrong. I thought it was a discussion but there was this Christian thing going on and I got talking to these guys and they said that as I wasn't a believer I'd be going to Hell. Pissed me off it did.'

'I'll bet it did.' I didn't know what to say. I looked at him twice, thinking he might be taking the mick. But, he wasn't. He was upset.

'Robert,' said Sidney, 'I'm a Christian and I'm telling you you're not going to Hell, there's no way man. It's not going to happen.'

'How the fuck do you know?' I could see why Robert was annoyed. With the best will in the world Sidney was no expert on something like this.

'I'm right, trust me.'

'But everybody's telling me I'm going to Hell. I was talking to this Muslim geezer and he said it as well. If I didn't say the prayers and do all that then I was going to burn in the fires of Hell.'

Nothing I had to say would do, but Sidney told him what his Gran had taught him and how his Gran wouldn't have anything to do with that sort of thing. She was a proper Christian. 'Nothing you've done man would get you into Hell.'

'It might.'

'No, it wouldn't. I know you man, you're not like that.'

And then of course the others started to make fun of the whole thing and what a fucking dork he was to listen to those tossers and how he ought to pay a bit more attention to Philosophy. Which was a bit unfair given that Robert always had star billing as far as I was concerned. He was really into John Locke he liked him for the notion that if you can't remember doing something then you can't be held responsible for it. Straight away he pointed out the possibilities this might hold for a defending barrister.

Joshua was stunned. He looked at me. He picked up his book.

'I'm keeping this book,' he shook it a couple of times, 'for my brief.'

I was willing to let it go, quite interested really to see just how far he planned to take it. How would the officers react? How would it go down if he has an adjudication? (A couple of years ago one of the chaps wrote to the governor and the governor began his reply with the words 'I see that you have been doing the Philosophy course…' It was a proud moment). But, Robert interfered and pointed out the absurdities and the consequences and I got to thinking again about this business of him being sensitive. Something must have happened. He reacted again when we got on to Locke's uncertainties about the nature of objects and I drifted off into Russell's Five Minute Hypothesis.

'There's no way that you can deny that everything, if that includes all your memories, came into being five minutes ago.' It just touched him on the raw, a raw that I'd never noticed before.

'What the fuck's that all about then? What was he doing, sitting having a shit, thinking, *This'll fuck the lot of them up?* It's into everything isn't it this Philosophy it just can't leave anything alone can it? The world, the world, it's just the world isn't it? It's not complicated.'

And I thought that I'd let it go, just for the time being. But then when the Protestant Ethic came up from somewhere and I told them a bit about the Glorious Revolution, Robert stood up and stripped off his T-shirt, turned, flexed, and there tattooed in big letters across his back was *No Surrender 1690*. Nobody else had the faintest idea what it meant and so he gave them a quick history lesson, which I must say was pretty good.

I was ready to lose Robert, in fact we'd been counting down from week ten. 'Nine to go Al, six to go, next week I won't be here.' It was this that was at the bottom of things, the fear that threads itself through the prospect of release.

'Have you got somewhere to live?' I asked.

'Yeah,' he said, 'got a room in a house, I'll be okay.'

'You must be nervous Rob.'

'I'm scared stiff; I'm always scared when I get out. What will I do? What will I do next Friday? I'll wake up and I'll think, "Yeah, Friday, Philosophy this morning," and I won't be able to come will I?'

Then it was next Friday and he had gone and so had Sidney and Spud and Raj and Josh. In fact there was only me and Ira left. Sometimes it happened like that, there's a clear-out and the men go home or off to another prison or they have to do a course with the psychologists: Offending Behaviour, Victim Awareness, Parenting, that sort of thing. It was all a bit melancholy, especially for Ira. Education Sue said that she had some new men lined up from induction and so I sat down with Ira and we planned what to do.

'Have you done any Aristotle?' I asked him.

'About a year ago,' he said.

'Plato?'

'No, that was before my time.'

'It certainly was.'

Chris had done Plato. Chris was one of Sue's new guys, just turned 50 and he'd had a big knock in his life. 'I'm alright now Al,' he told me, 'I'm clean, I'm eating again, doing exercise, putting some weight back on. It was such a relief to come to jail. When the door closed behind me I thought, thank God, thank God.'

He was the sort of guy I prayed to have in the Philosophy Class. I could set up a dialogue, pick arguments with him and because he had come across the ideas before he could beat me up a bit and that spread confidence through the room. It was always better when I was not the focus, not the teacher at the front. Ira knew the game and threw in ideas from Epistemology, which we were into a couple of months ago. It really cheered me up when I realised that they'd taken it all on board and that they could turn the ideas into new arguments. There we were with Ira in Plato's cave and it sent us off into a discussion about advertising and deception.

Chris told us about Utopias and let me in to talk about Dystopias. Alec chipped in with bits about Hitler and Stalin and Luke talked about English public schools and Plato's Guardians.

'What they're trying to do,' said Chris, 'is make us like bees , like ants, where everything's in order, everything has its purpose. But,' he said and he slipped it in so quietly, drawing all of us into his seriousness, 'we are not ants, we are men and for us things are complicated.' It left a short silence and I'm not sure that any of us were comfortable with this idea. Having a guardian to turn to would be a refuge.

'Or a Commissar,' said Alec.

'Yeah,' said David, 'or a Fuhrer.'

Then the morning had gone and we'd been a bit all over the place, which is fine by me.

'Do we have an exam in this?' Gordon asks.

Ira shakes his head, 'No bruv.'

'Well, what's the point of…,' and he saw Ira and me smiling.

'You ask that bruv and you're doing philosophy, that's what Robert would have said.'

'Who's Robert?'

'He used to sit there bruv,' said Ira, pointing at Robert's chair.

It set me off worrying about Robert's empty Friday morning. 'He should have been here,' I said.

'Yeah,' said Ira, 'maybe.'

It's hard to predict what will take wing. A few months later someone, I think it was Henry, asked about Existentialism and my heart sank. I've never been too keen on the Existentialists, a bit too over-invested in emotion I've always thought and I thought, too, that the class might find them a bit soppy. When something doesn't work with these guys not only do they make their feelings very clear but they also blame me. The Romantic Poets got very short shrift. Ahmed had looked at me accusingly when I'd given Wordsworth an outing. 'Al,' he said, 'he's a one trick pony.' I have never read him since.

However, we spent weeks with Sartre and in particular with the notions of facticity and bad faith. 'Not actually a lot of scope for free actions banged up in here, Alan.' Matthew being a bit rueful.

Luke, sounding offended, took him up on this: 'Hang on, I do a lot of things. Probably do too much.' He might have been right what with working with the handicapped kids, his OU course, being a Listener, Gym, Philosophy, Literature. Matthew himself had a full-time office job, classes in Philosophy and Business Studies and he seemed to spend most of what was left of his time reading Science and Politics. In fact, he was someone to whom I could hand over to from time-to-time when we got into one of his interests.

It was much the same for all of the guys in Philosophy. And Raymond, on top of everything else, was learning to be blind. They saw straightaway what an easy step it would be to let the prison, their facticity if you like, seduce them into bad faith. Easy to do nothing: sleep, watch TV, duck and dive, whine about the food, make excuses, retreat into fantasy.

Then we watched Endgame. I thought that it might be a bit insensitive, rubbing it in, considering where they were. They thought it was hysterical. 'Funny as fuck,' said Ted but I could see that it had left Brian a bit thoughtful and he started talking about the collapse of values. Then I mentioned the notion of Grand Narratives and eventually, this took weeks and weeks you understand, we got on to Marx.

Was it a good idea to talk about revolution in prison? Where better? I thought that Blake and the French Revolution might be a good way in. Blake never failed to take a grip: *Tyger, London, The Sick Rose*. 'Everything', said Arthur, 'contains the seeds of its own destruction.'

'He wrote Jerusalem,' says Ted and we stayed with that for a while and someone spoke about the legend of Christ visiting England.

'What!' said Ted, 'It's stupid.'

'No it's not.'

'Why shouldn't he visit England.'

'Oh yeah,' said Ted, 'imagine him at immigration? "Nationality?" "Palestinian." "Reason for visit?" "Building Jerusalem." "Profession?" "Son of God." Think they'd let him in? They'd jog him on straightaway.'

Brian, though is not put off. He starts to sing, 'And did those feet in ancient times…' and we join in. In the middle of the walls and the razor wire and the gates and the locks, bolts and bars, singing Jerusalem.

12

When Worlds Collide

The language in which all this happened could be quite startling. It was not the ordinary language of the Philosophy seminar room. Between prison and university I was going backwards and forwards between two quite different worlds. I think that most people who spend time in prison, staff and inmates, have this sense of a fractured life but I couldn't help but feel that I was getting a specialist version of this.

The university really was, and is, the nicest place I had ever worked in. The students always fell over themselves to be polite and co-operative. In their own, other-worldly way so did the students in the jail but the tiny, civilised island of Prison Education was set in a very difficult sea. Language was a rough indicator. I wasn't aware of it at first but the casual obscenity of the prison was following me into the university. My colleagues began to shy away. I began to measure my words, to pause before speaking and worry about what I was saying to the students. I could not stop swearing, saying the very worst things you could think of and often in ritualised combinations that left me breathless and appalled.

Our secretary in the prison, Helen, was openly distressed at the collapse of her own gentility. One of the guys came into the office to complain about the way some teacher had spoken to him. Helen had looked up from her keyboard and said to him, 'Oh just fuck off will you?' He was a bit dumbfounded and off he went. 'Do you know what I said to my husband last night?' Her eyes were downcast, she could not meet my gaze as she told me, whispering. It made me wince. She shrugged, 'Oh well,' she said, 'fuck it.'

I tried lecturing the guys in my class about not swearing in front of the lady teachers but they took it as a bit of fey irony and then, as they realised that I was serious, farce.

Thursday was the worst day of all. Thursday turned me inside out. On Thursday I worked in the prison and then, with only a brief drive between, I had a class at the university where I tried to impose a three second delay device, like a nervous chat show producer.

Why bother? When I read the first Creative Writing portfolios of my mild mannered undergraduates I was amazed that I had ever worried about their finer feelings. They should be locked up. Obscenity, casual and not so casual sex, drugs and decay, amoral violence and cynicism, Black Magic. It was the Girls Night Out genre that left me pinned back in my chair; it came up at me lipsticked and panting from script after script. These demure daughters of gentlefolk seemed, after dark, to be sexual banshees who dressed at Boutique Caligula. When term began, in they came simpering and smiling at me and offered all the polite deference of the nicely brought up. But I knew them now.

When he got out of prison later that year Stan had a university place to go to and I felt that I had to warn him about the robust hypocrisy that lay ahead.

'I can't wait,' he told me, rubbing his hands together in glee.

'What courses do these young women do? What they're interested in, I'm interested in.'

Rory chipped in: 'Trouble with English birds,' he said, 'is that they think they're lads.'

And they embarked on a startling conversation about the outer limits of sexual chaos.

'You, you sad old bastard,' Rory told me, 'you don't know what young girls are like nowadays.'

Afterwards Luke asked me if I had managed to read the stories he had given me the previous week. They were odd, beautiful stories about Luke's bedroom when he was a child; finding himself on the floor in the darkness, hiding from his brother's death. I'd also read Rory's heartbreaking account of his first days in prison, being helped through it by a distraught middle-aged man who had just killed his wife. Rory, who you might think would eat your liver, unable to forget his mum crying her eyes out in the court.

I sat in the office with Helen and we mulled over the inside-outness of it all. No good trying to judge people, we agreed and we shook our heads at the predicament our chaps were in.

'Why do they do it?' I asked.

'The silly fuckers,' said Helen.

After a while this resolved itself, became everyday and I just got used to living in two worlds. Both worlds became ordinary. This ordinariness is the worst thing about prison and I could see how those people who worked full-time in prison, not just the officers but anyone at all, could develop a resigned, cynical hopelessness. What I began, slowly, to realise was that my part-time life insulated me from this and it dawned on me that bringing the values of the outside into the prison was to my advantage. A typical prison view is that 'everybody's at it,' everybody is corrupt, vicious, self-seeking.

'Well,' I started to say, 'not in my street, people where I live aren't like that.'

'Yeah, but you've never lived on a sink estate.'

'Listen pal,' (yes, I had started saying 'pal' to people), 'where I grew up we aspired to living on an estate. We lived in crumbling Victorian slums. Don't think I had a silver fucking spoon in my mouth.' I got quite cross about this at times but in my heart I always knew that many of the men who were coming into my room had led lives of which I could only dream. It was and still is a shock to find men who were on the street before they were teenagers, men with histories of lives in care or at the mercy of violent feckless parents or worse. From a teacher's point of view it was a shock to find grown men, very intelligent men, with little sense of history or geography.

'I left school at eleven.'

'Thirteen when I left,' were not uncommon claims.

'How did you manage that?'

'Just did it. I reckon they were pleased to be shut of me. Nobody made much fuss anyway.'

Whether I was teaching Philosophy or Literature I was always teaching History. Simply getting things like Romans, Saxons, Normans in the right order can bring enormous satisfaction. History for many of the men was like a novel whose pages had been shuffled; they had stories and snapshots but nothing held together with any coherence. A common reaction is relief: 'Yeah man, I'd always wondered how that worked.'

They were often capable of asking those simple questions which made me stop and wonder sometimes what kinds of traps were being set for me.

'Al, what is Fascism, anyway? What does it mean?'

The sort of thing you think you know but then you have to struggle to get it straight. My students at the university were often wary of revealing scraps of ignorance but in the prison there was much more openness. They were like men in China, or somewhere exotic, who can't speak the language who realised that there was no point in pretending. The best thing was when someone they recognised from the wing someone like Mo or Pete who had enormous credibility could settle down with them and explain something: Mo talking about Economics and weaving in bits of Sociology and Politics or Pete on the slaughter of the First World War had an impact far weightier than I could have hoped for. I could slip out of my chair at the front and swop places with either of them and half-an-hour would pass by with the world turned upside down.

I began to work consciously at not being the only focus of authority and it was not always a popular move. This though was not ordinary Adult Education, this was a situation of such diversity of knowledge, experience and circumstance that my only durable option was to try to find a place inside it. Although, saying 'it' makes the situation sound like a single unitary whole where there was a place for me to find. The situation was always changing, not only when people came and went but also when some kind of a crisis blew up.

Things from the outside: children, marital upsets, family deaths and so on which would have anyway been dreadful and worrying would be brought into class in one way or another, intensified by feelings of guilt and powerlessness. Jenny and Gwen, working on schemes like Safe Ground, were making formal, self-conscious attempts to deal with this sort of thing and they worked hard at producing structures in which, for example, the griefs and guilts of being a father in prison could be faced. Teaching Philosophy and Literature left me a bit more exposed, left me feeling that I was a bit of a blunderer, left me wondering about what direction things might be heading.

Phillip Larkin, for example, was always a minefield and there he was a set text for A-Level. It's a pity that Larkin couldn't have done a few years in prison. He would have fitted in really well and probably enjoyed himself. The guys in my literature class really took to him. It might have been the direct, no nonsense sense of language, the booze, the porn and having three or four women on the go or perhaps it was just the courage and the honesty.

They liked his anger, the way in which he jumped up and down with it in *Sunny Prestatyn* and *This Be The Verse*. There is after all something, unmistakably, of the lifer about Larkin.

Not that he would have had too smooth a ride. Charles had the sense to pull me up when I was going on about *The Whitsun Weddings* and I could see that he and Larkin might well have had a brief but telling exchange back up on the wing.

'All that arrow shower crap at the end Al, it don't mean a thing; not after all the sneering he's done in the middle, manky little gett needs a bit of a dig.' Words mean something in the prison. Larkin would have had to watch his step with the racism as well, the guys won't have it. There might well have been a date with destiny in the showers.

When we read *Ambulances* there was no mistaking the real chill that Larkin put into the air. 'Very unpleasant that,' said Charles, catching in his own voice some of Larkin's sombre glee.

'Don't like to think of death like that, just being busy, being dead ordinary, in the middle of the street. Go off your head thinking like that.'

'He was off his head,' said Rory. 'See him on the telly?'

'That wasn't him.'

'I know it wasn't. I know it was a film. You mug.' Rory shook his head, 'Bottle of sherry for breakfast, course he was a bit off key.'

'Anyway,' said Charles, 'he takes a delight in it doesn't he, the miserable bastard?'

'Not in *An Arundel Tomb*,' said Charles, flicking through the pages to find the poem.

'Yeah,' Luke said, *They fuck you up your mum and dad*, that's not right is it?'

'Well,' said Charles, 'I can't say it is, can I? My mum and dad have been married for 30 years. Brilliant they are.'

Rory looked up from the book and said, 'Your mum's your best friend when you're in here.'

'Mine is,' said Lee. Every visit and she's here. Still calls me her little soldier. I try and tell her: I say, Mam I'm doing life, but it makes no difference. She's even stitched name tags in my clothes. I feel a right dick.'

'*What will survive of us is love*,' said Rory. 'Right at the end, page 46.'

He waited for us to find the place.

'That's true that I reckon. That's what he really thinks isn't it?'

Eric reached into his mouth pulled out his false teeth and put them on the table. There they were his four front teeth. Something had to be said and they were all looking at me. I suppose I was the teacher after all.

'For fuck's sake Eric,' I told him, feeling at a bit of a loss.

'Every night when I take my teeth out,' said Eric, 'every morning when I put them in, I think of my dad. He knocked my own ones out for me when I was a kid.'

'*Man hands on misery to man*,' said Eddy, in his soft Glaswegian whisper.

Eric's teeth glistened on the table. Eddy glanced at them. '*It deepens like a coastal shelf*', he assured us, smiling.

13

No Need to Sound Surprised

Charles appeared in my classes without any warning. He had the prison-gym build and a bit of a stare. Suddenly he was there. Like many of the new guys he came in and sat quietly, very still, hands clasped on the table in front of him and there was an air of melancholy and deliberation about him. I saw from the register that he lived up on the Lifer Wing and I knew that he must have been through young offender institution before Cat-B to get to us and still be so young. I asked him my standard question: 'Have you actually done any Philosophy before?'

'No mate.'

'Not got a degree tucked up your sleeve? Not going to show me up?'

'No mate. Did my GCSEs in my Cat-B.' He sat and stared, nodding slightly.

He came into English, a class where the guys were doing their A-Levels and had only about six weeks left before the exam. Charles seemed pretty okay with what we were doing and, in that spirit of 'Fuck it, why not?' that the guys sometimes go in for, I said, 'Why don't you do the exam? Just a few books to read and then you write about them.'

'You reckon?'

'Yeah, course you can,' said Rory. 'Christ, if I'm doing it..?'

'Yeah, alright then. If you put it like that.'

Like the rest of them he had a few nervous moments. 'Don't want to make a dick of myself. This is the first time I've done anything really difficult. Last night, this morning, it has not been good. I've been a bit trembly. Told some people on the wing I was doing this and they laughed. Told my Dad and I could see he was pleased.' But then, when the results came out he had a Grade B.

'Grade B in six weeks,' I said. 'What was all the carry on about, you big wuss.'

'Yeah,' he said, almost smiling. 'I have to confess, Al, I never actually read the Thomas Hardy.'

'But you wrote about it?'

'Well, yeah, actually. Piece of piss really. The others told me the story and I knew I couldn't be arsed with it. I sat down and I looked at the questions. I thought, fuckin hell, and then I thought, yeah, fuck it, I'll do the death one.'

When I'd got to know him a bit he told me, 'I was lifed-off on my eighteenth birthday, Al. My mum and dad; it was just terrible. You know what, when I was turned to go down to the cells the judge called me back.

I said, 'What?'

'I see it's your birthday today.'

'Yes?'

'Happy birthday.'

He was very calm about his situation but being in prison sat on him heavily. There was not much about him that seemed young and he would have flare ups of eczema and illness. I used to stand in the corridor with him after class, watch him walk off, hands in the pockets of his baggy jeans, heavy footed, as if there were a weight on his back. 'Be good,' I always said to him, it was what my mother always said to me.

Charles would turn and grin; 'Be lucky.'

When we persuaded Charles to do his A-Levels we had unleashed a monster. Sue, our new Education Manager, got him started with the OU and he did the Foundation Course. Nothing in all of Education gets even close to being as good as the OU's Foundation Course. As well as all the usual stuff Charles had to do Architecture and Music.

'What do I know about music?'

'Oh just do it,' I told him, trying to be impatient. 'Just stop whining.'

'Yeah, yeah.'

But, he did it and for a while he became an opera bore and then he told us several times all there was to know about the Roman Coliseum. He asked me if I knew anything about Viking mythology.

'No, what do you want to know about that for?'

'It's the only major set of myths I don't know.'

It turned out that he had spent years learning Greek, Roman, Indian, Aboriginal myths. Someone asked him to give a class about it and he was a bit of a spellbinder. There was a spot of difficulty in getting him to shut up when the three hours ran out. As usual when one of the inmates shows some talent, some knowledge, the other guys surround it with a bit of pride; it belongs to all of them. If I'm in the audience they nod at me, maybe point at the guy giving the class, 'See, see.'

I began to have a much more difficult time in Philosophy as Charles would take me over every word I said with a manic, finicky patience. At least this is what I accused him of. There was nowhere for me to hide and the class became something of a blood sport. Then I woke up and realised that I could go after him with the same sort of vindictiveness that had made Philosophy so enjoyable when I had been an undergraduate.

Being a teacher usually imposes a restraint, exacts a tolerance of the ways in which students blunder about. It really wasn't fair to go after someone who was just starting. The prison was, anyway, pretty robust but Charles, like Simon, set me free to say and do what I liked in class. No restraint needed, at least with him, as he seemed to be reading for about 18 hours a day and was clearly cleverer than me to begin with. It dawned on me that he was the one showing restraint; he was the one looking after my feelings. Bastard.

It was three years before Charles got his Cat-D and by that time he was well into his Philosophy degree. He was pretty sure that he would be going to an open prison in the south but, as always, nothing happened for a while then one day he had gone and it left quite a space.

'Be good,' 'Be lucky.' A few weeks later he rang up the Education Department and I spoke to him. He had the usual things to say about being in the open for the first time in his adult life: trees, the sky, stars, the difficulty with opening doors: 'Standing there like a lemon waiting for somebody to do it for me.' He told me about his outside job with the Royal National Institute for the Blind.

'Did I tell you I learned Braille when I was in Cat-B.

'What did you do that for?'

'Dunno, just did.' He could have done the exams with his eyes shut. Then he said, 'I've had an unconditional offer from the LSE.'

'No, you can't have.'

'I have.'

'You sure?'

'I've got the letter.'

'Jesus.'

'No need to sound surprised.'

'No, course not. You sure?'

'Course I'm sure.'

He had been called for interview and the academics had, naturally, offered him a place straightaway. Despite his OU modules he wanted to do three undergraduate years and they were delighted to have him. When he was released on licence we met up for lunch. This is the sort of thing that anyone working in a prison must absolutely not do; it can lead to all sorts of trouble. But, I had come to think of Jason as an academic colleague; someone I was going to bump into anyway at conferences and lectures over the next few years.

The academics, he told me, had made him the offer but then the people in administration had had a slight panic and they asked him to go in and speak to them about the situation. Their main concern was that they didn't see how he could live in a hall of residence. He had feigned innocence: '"Why not?" Course I knew why not. Couldn't have me next to an 18-year-old blonde child, could they? All home counties and pony club next to a lifer?'

In my view he would have been a good example, a model of modest behaviour and industry. 'So I said, "I think that you'll find that your letter constitutes a contract. You've offered me a place and your letter assures me that all first years are guaranteed a room in a hall of residence."' I knew it couldn't be done, obviously, but I thought I'd let them jump up and down a bit. They were very grateful in the end when I said, 'Yeah, alright.' But then, the cheeky bastards, this is how nervous they were of me, got frightened of the *Daily Mail*, I think. They said, 'Oh Mr. Wharton, there is actually one more thing, would you consider doing this course under an assumed name?' 'Yeah alright,' I said, 'put me down as Charley Bin Laden.'

When he began his course he didn't tell anyone about his history but he must have stuck out just a little.

'I reckon I've been sussed Al, bound to happen. The students union have asked me to run a self-defence course for the women students. God help anybody who attacks these girls.'

'You'll have to talk to your mother.' Charles's mother taught martial arts.

'I'm in her book you know.'

'What's that?'

'In the photos there's a really vile thuggy looking bloke who attacks her and gets flattened. That's me.'

By the end of the three years I think that he was fairly out in the open about things and when he began to publish in the academic press he just had to tough it out. After the LSE he went to Cambridge to do his MPhil and now he's into his doctorate.

In 2008, I went to Westminster to hear Charles speak, as a panellist, at the seventh Longford Lecture. At the pre-lecture drinks I spotted him, looking like a house side, black suit, shaven head. He came across the room like a train and put his arms round me.

'Here, Jon,' he said to Jon Snow, 'come and meet Al; taught me Philosophy in prison.' We smiled, both of us a little overwhelmed, I think, by the full sail of Charles' confidence.

Charles was on the platform with Dame Helena Kennedy, Sir Ian Blair (now Lord Blair) and Phil Wheatley the then Director General, National Offender Management Service. Jon Snow introduced Charles to the audience and wondered at the journey that his life had been. A life-sentence handed down on his eighteenth birthday and now here he was.

At the reception afterwards I bumped into his mother and father. For all those years they had never missed a visit, they had written piles of letters and never lost faith. Charles' dad told me about the visits; about seeing Charles with his face bust up after the continual fighting when he was in YOI; about Charles turning up with another lad who didn't get any visits so Charles had brought him along to share his. 'We had to visit this other lad as well. He's like that, Charles.' We were getting a bit close to tears and then Charles came and roughed us up a bit, taking the Mick, getting us to pose for photos with Jon Snow and scooping up more wine for us all from a passing waitress.

Charles's story is one in which I became involved because his academic interests were so like mine and when he was in prison we spent a good deal of time talking about Philosophy and Literature. He presents the world with an upbeat, positive attitude and his father says that he won't think about his years inside, only the future. We all know that this is not possible; perhaps it is one of those necessary fictions that get us through things.

Most success stories don't linger in my mind. The successes are, after all, simply a matter of somebody managing to have an ordinary life. The failures live on in my imagination. Failure is often melodramatic, particularly when it involves death, disaster, drugs, uproar, headlines, sentencing, outrage, horror. And so on. Charles's success is striking but for a man of his ability it is simply what might be expected.

14

Tossers Like Me

Luke's story had in it bigger achievements than that of Charles, but was shot through with dreadful disasters. A big factor in Charles surviving such a long period of imprisonment was that he had no history of drug use. Luke told me that as far as he could remember he had started taking drugs when he was about eleven years old. Most of Luke's life has been spent in care or in custody. I have met quite a few men like Luke and they always make me pause and reflect on my own story: the things that made me. Just think how things were for you when you were eleven. Being unhappy, having parents who were not very good, not liking school just doesn't compare with care, custody, the street.

Luke was in his forties, doing his eleventh sentence, when I first met him and he was often ill, often a bit withdrawn. He came into class to do his A-Levels, English and Sociology and his GCSEs at the same time. It sounds awkward but the men just did the courses which happened to be on the timetable at the times when they could get into the department. Luke was an intelligent man and he could write. He showed me a set of stories he had done and the Writer in Residence was quick to pick him up. When it came to writing essays, though, he had no confidence. And we had to bully and nag him into doing them. When he did them they were, of course perfectly competent and in the end he got his A-Levels.

He revealed, little-by-little, the plan that he had formed.

'I want to do some good, Al. I've done a lot of bad things. I mean, a lot.' And he would tell me appalling things about guns and drugs and knives and axes. Luke would sit with his head down, coughing up all this rancid stuff. He found his way onto the programme where some of the men worked with profoundly handicapped children from one of the local schools. 'You should come and see. I'll fix it up with Mr. Clelland.' I went and had a word with Willie Clelland myself and he was pleased that I was interested

When I walked over to the gym with Luke he said, 'I shouldn't be here really, I should be dead.' He looked up, sheepishly, and smiled a slight, innocent smile. 'This working with the handicapped kids,' he said, 'it was just thrown on me; it was part of the P E course. Nobody dropped out though; when the course was over, we all stayed on.'

There were eight of them, very quiet, serious looking men, getting out the mats, checking that everything was clean, nodding at me as they heard Luke giving me the details. 'Willie,' he said, pointing, 'Mr. Clelland, he will not let you piss about. You have to be genuine to get on with Willie, he's on the side of the children. He's a different bloke when he's with the kids, that's the effect that they have. I can see that now, now that I've worked with them myself, brings you down to reality. These kids they just struggle on, living it the best way they can and then there's tossers like me trying, the best way we can, to kill ourselves.'

I went and sat on the floor with Willie Clelland in the corner of the gym and he told me about what the men would be doing. Willie explained about the Sherborne Movement, how it needed a lot of staffing, one or sometimes two adults to each child to deliver the programme of touch, colour and movement. Luke had already told me a bit about this and about David, the little boy with whom he always worked.

'He's never even tasted food; he gets fed through a tube going into his stomach. I can tell now when he's okay doing stuff and when he's not. They were getting him to do stuff he wasn't up for and he got a bit upset.'

'I shouted at them "Now look what you've done," like he was my kid. Bit of a primitive reaction, surprised myself. When he first came, he came with a nurse, he was just out of hospital. He had a fit. I was going, "Is he gonna be alright. Come on David, breathe, breathe. Is he gonna be alright, is he?" What an eye-opener hey? How am I going to cope with this, I thought. It was a bit daunting.'

When the mini-bus arrived the men went out to greet the children. Willie didn't move. 'They know what they're doing,' he said. Outside the guys were waving, tapping on the bus windows, flattening their noses into funny faces through the glass. Dawn, a teacher from the school, was with them and she supervised the un-strapping and the wheelchairs until, at last, we were sitting in a circle on the gym mats. The men were cross-legged and the kids sat on their laps, they were all being rocked gently back and forth as Dawn checked that everyone was settled and that the men were aware of the various tubes and stitches they needed to be careful with.

The tiny girl on Cliff's lap banged her head in distress against his chest. He wrapped his massive arms around her and rocked her gently into quietness, whispering to her, 'They won't let you come to prison again if you don't behave yourself.'

Then we sang the hello song; we sang everyone's name and made thumbs up gestures. Then there was some really spectacular rocking with the men going almost head-over. Then the men tiptoed around the children keeping up eye-contact, toe-pulling, tickling. David had a fit and Luke sat stroking his head as Dawn talked him through. Luke looked around, sharply: 'Not his fault is it?' wanting, somehow, to defend the little boy. 'Have you finished? Good boy. Sorted.' There were donkey rides with the men being plodding monsters. Cliff's little girl lay, rapturously, against his back as he started to do slow press-ups, taking her up and down. There was blanket dragging and hammock swinging.

Jimmy crawled on his own into position for the next exercise, impatient and suddenly confident. The men lay face down tight up together and they rolled. The children were fed onto them like a conveyer belt and the little bodies surfed over the men, anxious, daring, delighted and the rollers cheered as they rolled. When David rolled his head went back but the man at the end was ready for this, caught him, gently, and cradled his head in the crook of his arm.

At the end of the session there was a big, round, multi-coloured canopy pulled out tight like a tent, circling above the children clustered at the centre of the mat. The colours went, suddenly, up into the air and the men dived in to join the children as the cloth floated down to cover them all.

After the goodbye song I watched Cliff putting socks and shoes on Anne's small, white feet. He picked her up in his big, body builder's arms. Her arm went round his neck and she took a tiny fistful of his blue prison vest. Luke was giving Daniel a high speed circuit of the gym in his wheelchair. 'She's got no sense of space,' Cliff told me. 'When she first came, about six months ago, she wouldn't cross the line on the gym floor, could have been a chasm on the other side for all she knew, but she's okay now.

The kids were back on the bus and there was more face pulling and waving.

'He's knackered.'

'They're all knackered.'

'See you later mate.'

I walked back across the yard with Luke and he told me: 'You've got to do this for the right reasons. Some think they can do this to look good for parole. We told them, forcefully, you're out of order. Yeah, very forcefully actually. More than two years I've been doing this; coincides with me shaking off the drugs. Makes you realise that, basically, you're in jail because you're an arsehole.'

Luke was driven by this feeling of his own culpability and worthlessness. Seeing him with the children was a contrast with the account he gave of his own life and demanded that someone like me took sides. Which Luke was I going to believe in? A silly dilemma, obviously but it was a response to the confusion I felt about Luke and often felt about many of the other men. Being a teacher, having a professional stance, does not resolve this confusion but it does present ways of acting which are pathways forward through this kind of personal mess.

From a teacher's point of view the next thing for Luke to think about was university entrance. He had considered this already and was, rightly, concerned about how he would handle it. In the end he decided that an Access Course at a further education college would allow him to find his feet on the outside.

Because he was a local man he asked me to contact the college. I was a bit concerned about this because it was where my wife worked and Access was a part of the department where she taught. I didn't have any misgivings about Luke but I didn't want to break any of the rules about being in contact with ex-prisoners. The rules in themselves are very sensible and, which was just as important from my point of view, not following them could have got me excluded from the prison. Teachers are employed by FE colleges who provide education inside prisons but the prison authorities have the right to exclude anyone from prison, which is, in effect, the sack. There is no reason to give any detailed reason for this: if they don't like you then out you go.

I put all of this to the back of my mind and telephoned Linda who ran Access. 'Oh that's all right,' she said, 'we've had chaps from prison in the past. No problem, let me send you the forms. When Luke came up for release he had a college place and a room in a house run by a charity which worked with ex-offenders. When he was released Luke had been drug-free for three years.

My wife worked in the college where he was doing his Access course and I saw him occasionally. One lunchtime when I met her in the college canteen I saw him sitting amongst a group of students and he came over and told me how he was getting on.

When he got out of jail and began his course he had had a big decision to make. 'We were in a Psychology Class that was about reward-based systems and I was revealing some, well, quite specialised knowledge. I mean, I've been on the receiving end of quite a few systems myself. Everybody else could use examples from their ordinary lives; all I could talk about was drugs and prison. I felt like a kid, a little kid. People were looking at me a bit sideways. So, I approached everyone individually. I made sure that everyone knew. It was fine, I didn't think it would be but it was. In fact', he gave me the big grin, 'in fact they elected me to be student rep on the college committee.' He saw the look on my face and pointed a warning finger, 'Don't take the piss Al, alright?' But he couldn't look me in the eye and put a hand over his face to hide, 'I was embarrassed, to be honest.'

Lynda beamed at me when I asked about Luke, 'He's a lovely lad,' she said. Right from the outset Lynda and the Access team displayed absolute confidence in him. Their attitude made a big difference even before his release. 'I had a head start,' he said, smiling, being a bit ironic, 'All that time I had to study, being in jail. But I know I'm up against it because of what I did. Now I've got to be a hundred and ten per cent sure, can't make a dick of myself. So, I read all the books. The other students tell me I'm a girly swot. My study-buddy calls me Saint Luke. "Stop it," she says, "you anorak, it's Friday night."'

He showed me a couple of his essays, they were covered with ticks and glowing comments. He was clearly getting on with the other people on his course; they were all aiming to go on to do degrees in social work. This was Luke's plan; to become a social worker and do some good, redress the balance of his life.

What made a big difference for Luke was the network of support that he found waiting for him at the college. When I saw him again he told me about where Linda showed him how to fill in the UCAS forms. 'What did they want from me? I had no idea. Lynda knew. Her confidence was my confidence. I was in a tiz about ticking the box for convictions. "Don't worry about that," Lynda said, "Universities are full of criminals." Then there was the personal statement: I had to sell myself harder than anybody else. Look, I've done all this, I know. But I'm the one who's got the scars. I've got the actual experience. I want to show them what they can never get from a book. So, I've got to get inside the language, use their complex language, move up a register. I'm managing to marry these bits of me together, the technical, sociological way of writing and the more naturalistic, subjective modes of discourse.'

I sat there with my mouth open. 'Modes of discourse?' I got a hard look. 'Yeah, well,' he said, 'don't laugh. Just don't. Right?'

At the end of the academic year we went to the college prize giving and there was Luke.

He was wearing a suit and he had an ID tag that said, *Luke Davies, Award Winner.* When it was Luke's turn the Principal read out the citation and then shook his hand. At the reception afterwards I caught Luke deep in conversation with the Vice Principal about the last meeting of the academic board. Luke was giving him a bit of advice about the sub-committee structure.

He asked me to speak to my colleagues at the university about his prospects of becoming a social worker. They asked him to come for an interview. Afterwards, he told me how it went.

'I was really concerned,' he said, 'when I got the letter. I'd been expecting the university just to take me. I'd got the A-Levels; I'd done the Access Course. Stupid really; they were bound to be worried about the serious offences. Have you seen my record?'

He pulled a plastic folder from his bag and handed it to me. There were pages of it, pages and pages.

'So, I thought, there's no point in beating about the bush; I sent them the lot. I had two doctors interviewing me, but they didn't harp on about how bad I'd been. They were just realistic about the kind of course I could do. Two doctors though. I tell you, I was nervous. I was thinking I ought to wear my suit: collar and tie job. But then I thought it was best to go as me: white T-shirt, jeans, polished my shoes.'

He shook his head. 'I've only just worked out why I was so scared. Every other interview in my life has been with the police; so you could say I was a bit defensive. Didn't sleep the night before, panicked all morning, going round and round getting together all the papers and documents I might need. Had to be sure I could make a case out. All I was missing was my brief. I froze up at the start of the interview; I thought they were doing hard cop soft cop on me. If two people are interviewing me, I start looking round for the tape recorder. But then they melted, I melted. They must have known the state I was in. Dr. Standen kept saying, "You'll be fine, you'll be fine,"'

When Luke started his course I didn't see him; his department was on a different campus from mine. When I did meet him again he looked terrible and he roped me in to speak for him at a disciplinary hearing. He hadn't been attending regularly and had been missing deadlines. He was ill, hepatitis, a legacy from his past, which would have been enough on its own but he was also adrift. Without the tight structures that prison and college had given him things had fallen apart. I suspected that he might have been using drugs again. Eventually he left the university and I saw nothing of him until there he was, on television, being arrested in a drugs bust. It was all terribly bleak.

What I ought to have done, I thought, was to have intervened in some way. I should have seen more of him, paid his rent, brought him home for tea, offered him the back bedroom, looked after him. I felt a bit of a shit. All sentimental nonsense. Luke's view, when he was in prison and clean, was that if drugs were involved then rules of normal conduct did not apply and there was nothing to be done. Only the individual involved could remedy the situation. It was a bit of cold comfort for me as I watched him being handcuffed on the local news.

In a few months time Luke found his way through the system and back into my Philosophy Class. He had had a five year break; the longest period of freedom in his adult life. He was nearly 50 and desperately ill. Because he took his chemotherapy on Thursdays he was too ill to come to class on Fridays. But, despite the awfulness of just about everything he made something of his twelfth period of imprisonment. When he was released he was well into his OU Sociology degree; once again he had worked with the children; once again he was drugs free.

He said to me: 'I've just got to have these walls around me.' It made my heart sink. Now he is free once more, but he will need some walls around him and I don't see where they will come from.

15

Seductive, Corrupting

Is it dangerous? That's what people want to know and I can see what they're getting at. Whenever prisons are depicted on television or in films it is almost always because a dramatic point of some sort is being made. Journalists and film-makers are not much interested in the ordinary, dull stuff which makes up most of prison life, most of any sort of life. Prison never felt dangerous to me, at least not after the original shock of the unusual wore off. I never felt unease at the prospect of going into work and why should I have? As a teacher I was always insulated from the worst of prison. The problem was that this sort of complacency could lead anyone, softly softly, into danger-ous or compromising situations.

One Thursday afternoon I was let into the prison and I went to draw a set of keys. There were none left, at least none that the rules permitted me to have as a member of the education staff, and I thought: 'Well, okay, I'll manage.' One of the security officers saw this, stopped me and gave me a good bollocking. 'You can't do that. How can that be safe?' and a good deal more. He was about my age, shrewd, very experienced. He knew where my classroom was and he knew that for at least part of the afternoon I would be locked in there with the guys. It was essential, in his view, that I had the means to get myself and the students out of the room in the event of an incident or an emergency.

So I went back and made a bit of a fuss and after a spot of paperwork was given keys from another group. I was pleased to have him looking out for me. It was easy for a bleeding heart liberal like me to forget that this was a prison, all too easy for me to be seduced by what went on in my classroom. After all, I got the guys who couldn't wait to talk about the Romantic Poets or compare productions of *MacBeth*; someone had to rub my nose in the fact that these chaps are not altogether typical and that when someone new started in the class, well, they could have done God knows what. He dropped in to see me again half way through the afternoon to bollock me again, just to make sure.

'That told you didn't it?' said Kenneth.

At the end of the afternoon I saw him again in the staff room. He was still on at me: 'You have to get things right,' he said. 'Remember where you are.'

It helped me to feel not quite a fraud when the 'Is it dangerous?' came up. I always tried to give the impression of modestly understated heroism, perhaps throw in a melodramatic story or two. A polite middle-class context like the senior common room was a good venue for this sort of thing. It worked best if I could have a conversation with someone about prison and just let the others overhear key, shocking bits. One of my colleagues, Lawrence, my university pal, had done some work with my groups when I was on holiday and he was always ready to make a bad impression on people. We had a whole load of new friends exclusively in common: armed robbers, drug dealers, grievous bodily harmers, murderers. It's not that the rest lacked charm but the armed robbers seemed always to have a blithe otherworldliness about them, a disregard for consequences. Oddly, they seemed to be the best storytellers and this might be why Lawrence took to them so quickly. Think of Long John Silver or Arthur Seaton or Falstaff; a good story can gloss over a great deal of awkwardness.

Our professor became quite concerned. 'Are there guards in with you?' she wanted to know. Guards, guards? What was she talking about? 'Is it dangerous?' What did she think I was? If it were dangerous I wouldn't have done it. There have, it's true, been a couple of times over the years when arguments have gone a bit too far. There was one time when I lost my temper and jumped to my feet and Sidney gave me that don't be silly look and calmed me down and one time when Wesley and Patrick did a bit of counselling on my behalf up on the wing. But, no, not *dangerous*. I've started to think, though, that prison might be seductive, corrupting. 'I'm not a scumbag Al,' one of the guys was saying, 'I don't go around stabbing people up,' and then he paused for thought, 'not unless they've pissed me off of course.'

And there I was nodding and saying, 'Yeah, well, fair enough.' And finding things funny.

'An axe,' one guy was saying, 'is a weapon.' We had been talking about how using tools might be a marker for intelligence and he was putting us right about the nature of axemanship.

'What,' said John, 'you hit him on the head with an axe?'

'I hit him everywhere, arms, legs, head. Chopped the fucker up. He fuckin' deserved it.' Well, it tickled me and over lunch I told the story to my wife and laughed. She thinks I'm barmy

And then there was Neil, I think he could see how I was teetering on the edge. He pretended, at least I think he pretended, to be outraged. 'What are you in for?' An innocent enough question (Unless you're a nonce of course).

'I'm a political prisoner,' said Neil.

'Thought you were in for drugs?' said Arthur.

'That's what I said.'

'What?' Arthur looked a bit perplexed.

'Yeah, that's right.'

'Bollocks.'

'Look, if I sell you something and you buy it, that's our business isn't it?'

'Yeah.'

'Nobody should interfere, should they?'

'Yeah, alright, alright.'

'So, the government comes along and interferes because it's got a political thing going about drugs. And, I, I, am the victim.' He was tapping himself on the chest. 'I, I am being persecuted. My freedom unreasonably interfered with.'

'It's scandalous Neil,' I told him

'That's what I think,' he said.

Of course, it was difficult to know if anyone meant a word of what they said, if I meant a word of what I said. I tried to talk to Lawrence about this but he was no damned use at all.

'Does it matter?' he asked. I thought that it did. I'd have liked a bit of certainty if only to reassure myself. Lawrence in his shifty literary way seemed delighted to lace together the dual unrealities of prison and the literary theory that he gave to the undergraduates. It doesn't matter, does it, if a narrative is true or not and anyway the author being safely dead then whose to know?

He told me that we were in the 'Interpretive Community' of the prison and gave every appearance of knowing what he was talking about.

Philosophy never really exposed the differences between my middle-class university world and the world in which at least some of my prison students lived. It was in the English Literature Classes, and especially when we were reading Shakespeare, that the desperate lives that some men had lived were revealed. Not simply revealed but appealed to and articulated.

Eddy was in his forties, a quiet, self-effacing Scotsman, a polite person, very considerate. He had come to class looking, I think, for something to do to pass the time and he found us reading *Henry V*. What really pulled him in was the slaughter at Agincourt, the neatness, the cleverness of it. Those longbowmen, working-class guys armed with skill and muscle against all those hi-tech aristocrats and bringing them crashing down. Then, going forward with daggers drawn, maybe the knives they ate with, lifting up the visors and finishing them off through the face.

'Quite fucking right,' said Eddy. He ordered books from the library and read up on the battle and then learned all about the longbow: the different woods and grains and then the hours of practice and the simple, loyal stoicism of the bowmen. It drew Kenneth in too. They sat together and nodded their way grimly through the play.

Kenneth, who had way back in his youth been something of a football hooligan, had a sudden eye-flashing moment of empathy. He stopped me and asked me to read it over again out loud, that speech before Agincourt:

> We few, we happy few, we band of brothers;
> For he to-day that sheds his blood with me
> Shall be my brother ...

He went back and read all of that speech yet again. He looked up.

'We were in Scotland once, for an England game, and we were besieged on a traffic island. Two or three hundred of us and all these mad Jocks baying for our blood. One of the London lads, he got up on one of the bollards and made this speech. "Right, you bastards," he said, "this traffic island, this is England, right, and we are not giving it up, we are not running away. Right? Right?" He went on and on, ranting at us. Everything in you wanted to run, my heart was bubbling away, but he'd made his speech. When they charged they were gibbering for blood, but there was an instant, just an instant, when we stepped forward, when they saw that we weren't going to run and they paused. That was it, just that instant and bang we were on 'em. We happy few, man, we band of brothers.'

Then we got into reading the Roman plays. Eddy read *Titus Andronicus*, saw the film, and that started the ball rolling. I was a bit worried about how the guys would cope with reading their parts but they just plunged in. One was so enthusiastic that even reading Brutus wasn't enough and he started mounting takeover bids for the Soothsayer and Calpurnia when Brutus wasn't around.

'What you doin', that's my part that is.'

'Oh, OK, sorry,' and the sheepish, insincere grin. The mixture of accents– London, Caribbean, Scots, African — changed the text somehow, relocated it. I saved Eddy for the part of Antony, wondering what he'd do with it. He spent the week between classes going over Act Three in his pad, rehearsing. Eddy had a slow, Glaswegian voice, edgy and ironic and that's how he read Antony. No histrionics, no big moments, just a vicious, street-inflected whisper and the sense to let the verse look after itself.

> O, pardon me, thou bleeding piece of earth,
> That I am meek and gentle with these butchers! Brutus — How much trouble is
> he in then?

Antony with a hammer and a sawn-off under the folds of his toga. At the end of the act we took a break.

'You could have warned me about 'Ate',' Eddy said to me, clearly annoyed. 'You've no idea how much trouble I've had finding out if it was one or two syllables. It's no easy to find out something like that in a jail.'

'Just make it scan,' I told him. I got a bit of a look.

Then Kenneth chipped in, 'I get really annoyed when I can't get this Shakespeare stuff straight off.'

'You've got to study it,' said Eddy.

I think they quite liked the academic points that I made about the text. They extended to me the kind of polite tolerance they'd give to a Martian.

What really gripped them is what the characters did and how ruthless or feeble, vain, bloodthirsty or devious they were.

They saw straightaway, instinctively, that Roman politics was the politics of the street. The Roman plays succeeded in ways that the tragedies missed. The guys liked the ethic of no whining and no excuses that pervaded them. If you screwed up, then you blamed yourself and whacked your sword up under your ribs. In Rome, just as in the jail, it was the stoic who commanded respect.

There was a quite worrying amount of identification going on when we read *MacBeth*. Kenneth threw the book down and said, knowingly, 'He's just a geezer isn't he?' They rather liked MacBeth. So, okay, the MacDuff business was a bit out of order but the rest was fair enough. He should have got rid of the dippy wife though. They certainly approved of his fuck you attitude at the end of the play and rather than seeing it as a final playing out of tragic inevitability they thought it was a stylish flourish, a faithfulness to what he was. In the end he was only brought down because of a dirty trick.

Everybody had to start from scratch in jail; Shakespeare, Milton, Heaney, Larkin, everybody. These were readers who came without the usual critical paraphernalia and so came to some fairly brisk judgements. Hamlet: 'what a prick.' Antony: 'pussy whipped.' Othello: 'Fuckin' idiot.' Cleopatra: 'Slapper'. I had never had much time for Post-modernism before but now I found it a refuge and a comfort. Any kind of dispute could be resolved by saying something like, 'Yes that's an interesting reading' or 'There's no reason why those two readings can't exist simultaneously.' In fact it was the spontaneous, complete agreement about Faustus that took me by surprise. He met with universal approval. 'That's just like me,' said Patrick, 'Of course he wants things. What's wrong with that? Temptation and seduction aren't good or bad they're just normal.'

They all agreed that Cornelius and Valdes should be played by women so that they could really seduce Faustus, really make that connection. There was, too, complete agreement about Antony and Cleopatra.

'Antony's a fool,' said Tim, 'there's only Enobarbus in it. They should rename the play Enobarbus. Why does Antony go chasing off after that old slapper?'

Wesley looked up, straight-faced, and put the play to rest forever, 'Cos she fuck him like a bitch,' he said, knowingly, and we could only nod in agreement at this simple, elegant resolution.

When Eddy found out about my books he said that he'd get them out of the library and tell me if they were any good.

This sort of reaction was there again when we read Yeats. 'Are we gonna do this or what?' Kenneth said. He picked up the book and shook it at me. 'W B Yeats, any good is he?'

'Yeats?' I said, 'Kenneth, he's the best there is,' and we made a start on *The Second Coming*. It blew them away and me with them and the last thing on any of our minds was jail.

The poem led us into talking about religion and Kenneth smiled and said. 'This Easter will be the last big festival I spend in jail.'

'That's definite is it?' I asked him, 'you'll be gone before Christmas?'

'Yep, I can go to mass on the out this Christmas.'

'What am I going to do on Thursdays if you and Eddy leave?'

'Can't expect us to stay, Al.'

'Come on Kenneth, that's a bit selfish.'

Kenneth was an altar boy and served mass when the priest came in. His Christianity left me slightly bemused and I always had a bit of a go at him about the rackety life he'd had and he always explained that without his religion he would have been infinitely worse than he was.

'Keeps you in check does it?'

'Sure does,' he told me, without a breath of irony.

We took a look at *An Irish Airman Foresees his Death*. The guys were fascinated by the sheer deadly recklessness in the poem. Their own careers as warriors lead them straight to *A lonely impulse of delight/Drove to this tumult in the clouds*.

'You've been there have you?' asked Kenneth, 'when you think, this is it I'm gonna die.'

'Yeah,' said Eddy, 'and you just think, well fuck it.' Every head in the room nodded, except mine.

It all made me think about those Elizabethan writers, the desperate lives they led as soldiers, sailors, plotters, fighters and poets.

Kenneth and Eddy lived in different parts of the prison and so they only saw each other on Thursday afternoons. They had a compartmentalised, arm's length friendship and would sit and nod agreement as they listened to each other speak. I would often sit quietly and listen. It was a bit like being an anthropologist invisibly embedded in a strange tribe and I would try not to blunder around. This, of course was going on in reverse too and I would feel their curiosity focussing on me as I spun out something about Roman politics or analysed a bit of text. Someone might say: 'Do you think that was deliberate?' when I'd suggested a range of meanings for something and I could get them to spend half an hour wondering what 'deliberate' might mean.

'You're fuckin' mad,' Kenneth would say, laughing, the strange tribe that I came from as much a curiosity as theirs was for me.

For some time I had been having odd conversations with Eddy about writing. Like quite a few of the guys he wrote poetry. Most of them simply dashed down how they felt about things in the most dramatic words that they could find or searched around for clunking rhymes. Now and then something good would come along, but only now and then.

What was usual was an impatience with the notion of carefully crafting something and then rewriting. In fact this was often denounced as contrived and false, a betrayal of the real life business of making your feelings plain. Eddy, on the other hand, was really interested not in making his feelings plain but in having an effect, in imposing himself upon the world. He did have, after all, quite a history as a fighter and just as fighting involved knowing what you were doing, like Henry's archers, he saw straight away that writing demanded some calculation. He kept his writing in a big, stuffed, ramshackle notebook.

One afternoon I found myself with just Kenneth and Eddy. It was one of those times when the other guys had been siphoned off into appointments with probation or visits or had been sentenced to a spell in Seg. Eddy had the notebook with him, it was on the table and he was leaning forward, hunched, with his arms on his big bundle of papers.

'What's that? Kenneth said.

'It's my journal.'

'What's that then?'

He was staring at Eddy, his face bright with false innocence, just dying to draw Eddy out.

'It's where I write stuff.'

'What sort of stuff?'

'All sorts.'

'What all sorts?'

Eddy's head was down. Kenneth had pushed him back a bit and I could see that he was wondering what he could safely offer to shut Kenneth up. He had brought the writing with him for a reason but the dangers were only now becoming plain.

'Well.' Eddy paused, looked at me, smiled, looked at Kenneth and you could see the bright idea dawning across his face.

'There's my rules for life.'

'What are they then? said Kenneth. 'Are there many?'

'Oh there's 20 odd.'

'Go on then, give us one.'

Eddy put his hand up, pushing us away, making a bit of space for himself. He opened the book and, slowly, found his place. Kenneth folded his arms on the table looking like a kid waiting for 'Are you sitting comfortably ... '

'Rule Eight,' said Eddy, 'never stab anybody in the neck or the chest.'

I put my head in my hands, 'Fucking hell Edward.'

'Yeah, that's a good one,' said Kenneth and they nodded at each other.

I couldn't help it: 'Why not?' I said, 'Wouldn't that be effective?'

There was a moment's quiet. 'If you stab someone in the neck or in the chest,' said Eddy, explaining things slowly to the idiot and pointing to neck and then chest, 'you will kill them.'

'And then,' said Kenneth, slowly, explaining, 'you will get life.'

'And,' said Eddy, 'you don't want that, now do you?'

I knew that they were taking the piss but I was flustered by this sudden drop into the hole. On the other hand, I was interested. 'Go on then, where would you stab someone?'

'In the arse,' said Eddy.

'Or the face,' said Kenneth.

See,' said Eddy, 'If you stab someone in the arse,' he stood up and mimed it, 'ah! ah! then it hurts like fuck and there's blood all over the place. Terrible messy. Scares the guy to death and he falls down or he fucks off at high speed. Fight over. No harm done.'

'In the face,' said Kenneth, 'Same thing. Just there in the cheek. It's a really, really shocking thing to happen to you. Soon as the guy feels the blade on his teeth he panics. Fight over.'

He looked at my face. 'Don't want to hurt anybody Al, just want to get the thing out of the way.' Useful to know, that kind of stuff, and if ever I get in a fight then I'll know just what to do.

Where else in the world but our Literature class could Eddy, Kenneth and I meet? Where else could there be such conversations when there was nothing standing between us? They were not sneering at me for being soft and I was not falling back on my cushion of morality. No-one was frightened; there was no affront, no judgement. All three of us felt how odd it was.

16

Money Well Spent

Across the corridor from my teaching room was the most popular class in the prison. Debbie ran Cookery Classes and the guys could eat what they made. It was a room where there had to be a lot of confidence; there were all those dangerous things that you have to have in a kitchen. The door was kept locked and the guys were always searched as they left at the end of a session.

One morning there was a rather good-looking lady officer doing the rub downs and a dozen guys lining up to be searched. She was just getting on with it but it started to occur to her that the job was taking a lot longer than it ought, that she had searched an awful lot of men. Well, of course; the guy she had just searched was going to the back of the queue so that she could search him again. It was the giggling that gave them away. They made her blush.

'Bastards,' she told them, laughing at their cheek to herself, 'bunch of bastards.'

They wouldn't have tried it on with Debbie. Debbie was a tiny blonde woman who treated the guys like naughty boys and she attracted a lot of loyalty, everyone knew what efforts she made to keep the Cookery Class afloat. Normally she had one or two self-appointed minders who always looked as though they might fillet and eat anyone who drifted out of line.

Debbie used to cook for millionaires, in fact Debbie used to cook for the Queen on the Royal Train. Her budget in the prison was a little more limited. Her cooking here in the jail is done on 60 pence a head.

'Not a lot is it?' she said, 'and that includes everything: laundry, washing up liquid, the lot.'

Debbie's Domestic Science room is spotless. 'It's got to be hasn't it. That's lesson number one, everyone cleans up their own mess'. The room gleams. 'Every few weeks I can run to a bit of chicken for the lads and you've just come in on the right day; chicken tikka and Bombay potatoes today and a bit of shortbread.' She showed me a plate of chicken. 'Fifteen of them this morning, they'll not get fat on that will they?'

The guys were starting to arrive, picking up their pinnies from behind the door. 'Do me up will you?' said Arnold.

'Come on then,' Debbie was rounding them up, 'Get your hands washed.'

'Washed them Miss,' they told her and held up their clean hands, teasing.

'Come on, come on, demonstration.'

Everybody was focused on her as she went into TV chef mode. Danny stood half a pace behind her, muscles rippling in his pale blue prison vest. As she finished with a dish or spoon he stepped smartly forward, clearing up the waste bits, washing up as she went. He stepped back into position.

'Now, I'll just get Danny to rub this pastry mixture up for the cherry short-bread.' Danny was at her side rubbing away in the flour and marge, using just his fingertips, as delicate as can be. 'I'm just skinning the chicken…' Someone was talking… 'you do want to come to cookery next week do you?' She softened the threat with a little smile and poked out her tongue. 'Thank you.' She had Danny frying onions. 'When the spices are cooked out we put in the potatoes.' She glanced at Danny, in went the potatoes. 'Right then, queue up for your stuff.'

It struck me what a dangerous place the cookery room might be as the guys went off to their work areas carrying knives and rolling pins. The door did have a separate alarm system and there were searches, but like so much else in the jail's Education Department the Cookery Class depended on the fundamental decency of the men who came to us.

Danny was rolling his pastry, he gave it a gentle pat as if to congratulate it for being so perfect, cutting the biscuit shapes and making the edges just so with the point of his knife. Debbie brought me a coffee and a hot biscuit, one that Danny had made earlier. We laughed at Arnold who was making little faces on his biscuits.

'They look a bit glum,' I said to him, 'curl the lips up a bit.'

'These are prison biscuits,' he told me. His mate Jack was making up a bowl of tikka mix.

'Cor that looks good,' Debbie said as she stuck her nose into it and came up smiling. 'Do you want a drop of yoghurt for that?'

'Please.'

While the chicken was marinating Jack sat and talked to me. 'I'm in here for cannabis growing.'

'Ridiculous.'

'Course it is.'

'When I lived in Holland I won a trophy for it, over here I'm locked up.'

'You won what?'

'A big silver cup. The little town I lived in had a Gardens and Produce Show and I won a cup for my cannabis plants. Only thing I've ever won in my life.' We both looked down at Arnold's cooling biscuits, thinking about what would really improve them.

At the next cooker Hector and Perry had branched out into West Indian dumplings and they let me scrounge one.

'Where'd you learn that?' I asked.

'I didn't have to come to prison to learn to cook, my mum taught me. At the age of ten I could cook iron and wash; anything a woman can do for me.' He paused, a faraway look suddenly in his eyes. 'Well,' he said, 'almost anything.'

Jack stood over the frying pan, fork poised, nibbling a bit of Bombay potato. 'I declare this cooked.' He served up the chicken tikka for himself and Arnold arranged the food nicely on the warmed plates.

'Smells nice,' said Arnold.

'This chicken,' said Jack, fumbling it in his mouth because it was hot, 'is superb.'

'Beats what we get on the wing,' said Arnold.

Debbie came and sat with us and told us about spices, about how just a little of the ginger brings out all the others. There was something very domestic in the air as the guys ate the lunch that they had made for themselves.

'This morning's meal came in at 59 pence,' announced Debbie. 'We should do a book about how to live well for pennies. A lot of these guys will be starting from zero when they get out you know.'

Arnold served up the glum biscuits and then there was a bit of a sprint to do the dishes and clean the place up before the officers arrived to search the guys at the door. Everything got a good scrubbing. 'Better than we found it,' said Danny.

'There's a rolling-pin missing.' Debbie said, banging cupboard doors.

'Is that it down Perry's trousers?' asked Hector.

The cookery room was the most calm and domestic environment. There is, anyway, something human and comforting about food but the juxtaposition of the kitchen and the often oppressive maleness of the prison made cookery a place to breathe more easily. This was a low intensity, civilising, purposeful place where the simplicity of food produced a small sense of community, mutuality, gentleness.

The cookery class was closed down and the kitchen equipment taken away. Somebody, somewhere, on a big fat salary I suppose, couldn't see the point of it, didn't think that the 59 pence was well spent.

17

Look at All This Then

The first Art teacher I met was Glenn. Glenn's problem was that he was forever being mistaken for a prisoner and he would get lots of hassle from officers new to Education. His jeans and T-shirt way of dressing, his 'Awright, Guv' accent, and No.1 haircut made it inevitable. I had been a bit surprised at first by the absence of a prison uniform. Whilst there are standard, prison issue clothes, generally speaking no-one is obliged to wear anything in particular. Ahmed told me that this was because of the IRA. 'The IRA lads,' he explained, 'refused to wear prison uniform because they reckoned that they were prisoners-of-war, not criminals. So, there was a bit of a stand-off and to avoid the issue the government said that everybody, IRA or not, could wear what they liked.' Which solved their problem and created Glenn's.

After five years of this it was time to give all of his energy to his new business empire. The tattoo parlour and fetish clothing shop had really taken off since he moved to Kettering and he wanted to be in the spray on multi-coloured latex and leather full-time. I think though that there was also a slight psychological crisis. It started with his first tattoo, just a small tasteful affair at the top of his left arm, nothing figurative, but something that harked back to South Sea warriors and Winchester School of Art.

The tattoo sub-culture in the nick embraced him, blue armed, as one of their own. We watched helplessly in the staff room as the tattoos rolled down his arm reaching in vivid tongues of yellow and red fire towards his wrist. He became a tattoo snob; Brian Sewell could not have been more contemptuous of the tattoos that some of the lads flexed at him and I think that he was genuinely upset by some of the DIY efforts, crude stuff, done with a pin and biro ink. He was more interested in working out really good designs in the Art Room which could be, perhaps, translated into tattoos when release came along. When he opened his first tattoo parlour I am sure that it was in reaction to a setback in his Art teaching.

'I am,' he told me, 'completely pissed off. Some of those guys have been in my class for months, years some of them. I asked them for examples of painters they liked. Nothing. Silence. Do you know what they came up with in the end? Johnny Hart and Rolf Harris.' Even if they were teasing it was a cruel thing to do. After that he took to wearing sleeveless T-shirts which showed off his arms and the tattoos started to fill his back and chest. Now, Glenn really was an artist, he had won a scholarship to the *École des Beaux-Arts*, The Sorbonne, and if you really want to be tattooed he could well take you to the Tate Modern end of the market, although you will inevitably run the risk of art theft. I don't know if I should mention this to the class he left behind, but if you could just catch him and skin him…

He made me wonder what working in the prison might be doing to me. If he, young and talented, went from *École* to latex and labial tattoo work in a few short years, what could be lining itself up for a clapped out old hack? Does the Ministry of Justice have a duty of care, would they be responsible for my descent into the pit. Could I take them to court? Could Glenn?

Sue, on the other hand, Pottery Sue as the guys called her, was altogether far more indestructible. She had the Essex accent and just the right amount of in-your-face belligerence to make the extraordinary things that happened in her workshop seem possible. She was a good looking woman but she was old enough to be the mother of most of the guys and, in some cases, their grandmother. Sometimes they forgot and called her, 'Mum', and, as she said, you didn't know whether to laugh or cry. Like your mother might well have been she was, for part of the time at least, an unreasonable nagging presence but she never ran out of patience with the guys and would make all sorts of things possible. Raymond was a good example of this.

Ray was in the middle of a longish sentence when, one morning, he woke up and he couldn't see. He had been headachy for a few days and then there he was being rushed to the hospital for brain surgery and then he was back in the jail and 90 per cent blind. Patrice brought him to Philosophy and he got on like a house on fire; he didn't have to read anything and he could argue the toss as well as anyone else.

Later on I was in the Education office talking to Patrice and Henry and we got onto Ray. 'First time I met him,' said Patrice, I was going past the chapel and Rachel the Vicar called me over, asked me to take him back to G Wing, which sounded a bit strange, but I said, " Yes fine." Then, because he hesitated, I took his arm and turned him onto the stairs. I almost threw him down them and he clung on and he said, "Hang on mate, I don't see much; I'm blind." Christ I'd nearly killed him. Back on the wing I started to notice how he was struggling—you should see Ray getting hot water from the boiler, it's terrifying. He wasn't doing anything, you know, wasn't getting out of his cell. So, I mentioned it in Education and Sue got him started.'

'He went to Pottery first,' said Henry, 'Now he's everywhere.'

I liked it myself in Pottery and so if there was any excuse for a visit I was there. As soon as I got in the door they started on me. 'Here, you wanna buy a pot mate. I'll put the handles on it for you if you like. Look at that, nice pot for your vinaigrette. Tenner?'

'Joseph,' said Pottery Sue, 'leave him alone. If you want Ray,' she said to me, 'he'll be here after movement. You heard what happened to him because of the painters? Over the weekend they painted everything cream, looked a treat it did but it buggered Ray. I found him stood in the corridor panicking in a big cream glare. Sheila, you know, the principal officer who looks after him, she went bonkers, got them straight onto it dark edging all the steps and doors and skirtings.'

'She got him a talking watch,' said Scott, 'it tells him the time every hour, all through the night. Going crackers 'cos it keeps waking him up.'

'Can't he turn it off?'

'There's an instruction booklet, not much good to Ray though is it?'

'What about an egg rack?' said Joseph, 'Fiver. Shouldn't keep your eggs in the fridge you know.'

Then Raymond came in.

'Ray,' said Joseph, 'he's just turned my egg rack down.'

'Can't fault him there,' said Ray.

He folded up his stick and sat down at the table in front of the black laminated work surface that Pottery Sue had made for him. 'She got me into it, he said. She came up to see me in my cell. I thought, smashin', I've got a woman in my cell.'

'Then he realised it was Sue,' said Scott.

'Cheeky bugger,' said Sue.

'So, I said to her, "Yeah, I'll give it a go. I was pleased, Alan, I mean, I couldn't go to Employment, I'm too much of a risk. I'd nothing to do.'

'I started him off rolling coils with his hands on mine,' Sue told me, 'so he could learn by touch, but he just picked it up; he's an easy student to teach.'

'Anyway,' said Ray, 'do you like my bowl?' And I did like it. It was a shallow scalloped affair in bright, piercing white. 'I'm gonna put it on the little turntable and pour a fine line of blue into it and let gravity create its own spiral.'

'I think you get a bit frustrated though, don't you?' said Sue.

'Yeah, I do,' said Ray, serious for once, 'and since the operation I reckon I've got a bit obsessive. Everything's got to be neat and tidy, everything squared away.'

'And then,' Sue said, 'I have to dive in and sort him out.'

'Should've seen it when the inspectors were here,' said Scott.

'Oh yes,' said Ray, full of enthusiasm, 'that lady inspector, I drew her right in. "Come over here and help me with this." I overwhelmed her. She didn't know what to make of me.'

'Tell you what,' said Joseph, trying to sound inspired. 'My entire collection: 35 quid. Best offer.'

'It's a bit silly, don't you think, keeping him in jail?' said Scott.

'No,' said Ray, 'I'll do my bird like everybody else. No complaints. But, you know, I'm doing it in prison and I'm doing it in my head.'

'Once for the body, once for the soul,' said Joseph and we all turned and stared at him.

Once I'd started going into the art room it was hard to keep away. It was one of those places that was nothing like prison and yet it was only possible to have this other world against the background of the prison machine that was just outside the door.

'They take this very seriously,' Sue pointed at the four pots on the workbench top. 'Monday morning and there's queues of them sick with worry. They have sleepless nights at the weekend, wondering if the pots have blown up in the firing.' She points at the four pots on the table. 'These are great. Have you felt them? Feel that.'

We all trace our fingertips along the curve of the glaze.

'A lot of guys send stuff home. You remember Frankie? When his father died he was given permission to go to the funeral. They took the cuffs off so he could walk behind the coffin. He made a pot and did some really good engraving on it: cherubs and angels chasing around with harps and trumpets. Classic. His dad's ashes are in it now, in his mum's house.'

'Have you seen Terry?' said Ben, and I could see that he was impressed. 'He's doing a life-sized alligator.'

Terry was circling, dancing, around his alligator's head. He walked away and was looking at it from across the room as if he were hunting it down. Then he had his fingers in its teeth, wrestling it like Tarzan. Then paring slivers of clay from it, hardly seeming to touch the surface.

'Del does coils,' said Sue, 'fabulous."

'Go away,' Del said, 'you making me all shy now,' blushing under his dreads. 'Can't throw can I? It goes all over the place. Look, see this one, first time I've been able to engrave on coils.'

Then he nodded me away; 'Look at Dave on that wheel, man. Yeah, he's an animal ain't he?' The wide slab of David's back was bent over the wheel and his diver's boot of a foot click-clicking delicately on the pedal. Sue was telling him, 'Nice and relaxed, you don't want pressure on it, it'll go all wobbly.' Dave's nose was two inches from the pot, lost in concentration.

Neil had spent all morning using the tip of a fine brush, working on his elephant, hardly moving, his face, focused and intent. 'Don't make him jump, for God's sake,' Ben whispered to me.

Later Neil showed me some of his other pieces. He opened the cupboard door and there was his menagerie. 'This is the best, a mandrill. I struggled to get the hair texture on the legs; the texture on the back though, that's just right.' And it was. He shook his head: 'Tried and tried to get rid of that smile, couldn't get rid of it.' Then he reached back into the cupboard and showed me, flat on the palm of his hand, the tusks for his elephant.

Ivory?' I guessed.

'No mate, it's soap. Terry done 'em for me. Brilliant innit?'

'All this is a bit of a shock for these guys,' said Sue. 'Mostly they've led pretty tough lives and then they have to face up to this side of themselves as well.' She said it so that they could all hear. She was telling them what they thought. Was it odd, telling people what they thought? I made a note for the Philosophy Class.

Roger was nodding: 'When you're outside you're just pushing into life, no time to think about things. On a sentence there's time to reflect on things; that's the way I took it.'

His face fell. 'A short sentence, though, I only had a short sentence. Not like my pal Will.'

He pointed at the end wall. 'See my picture?' There was a romantic landscape of lake and mountain, trees, flowers and sky. A prisoner's landscape. Then in the corner I spotted Will where Roger had set him free. Will, sitting in a meadow. 'Yeah,' said Roger, 'I made him young. He's a bit old now so I gave him back some years. Put a bit of hair back on his head.'

The animals got a bit out of hand and in the staff room Sue kept on and on about how the menagerie was taking over. A few weeks later I found her packing them in big cardboard boxes: the elephants and the bear, the Egyptian cats, the pink tongued dog and the monkeys. The two crocodiles were a bit on the big side to be sent through the post and Neil's gorilla was waiting for the flesh to be put on its bones.

'We've got the chance to exhibit at the Arts Centre at Leyhill Prison,' said Sue. 'It really focuses the lads something like this. Lets them find the best in themselves. I don't want the elephants to go though, I don't, it'll break my heart.'

The elephants, that were small enough to stand on your hand, were the first things that Neil ever made, but then he moved on to bigger things. The gorilla for instance. When I asked him about it he went, without a word, and got it out of the cupboard and put it in front of me. It was a skull. It sat there, with its blank, untouchable, stare like a piece of heavy engineering: the indifferent weight of the jaws, the arrogant, dead weight. Neil left me to it and was focused on his current figure, a tiny thing that could stand on your palm, it had him spellbound. He turned it this way and that on the wheel putting in texture of hair and skin with fine wire tools and an old steel nib.

'It's a woman', said Sue, speaking softly in my ear. I could see what she meant in the sensual, hidden shapes in the groin and the belly and the fine, vulnerable fingers held against the weight of the head.

'Is it a woman Neil?' I asked him.

'Dunno.'

'What do you call it then?' He glanced at me, said nothing. 'If you were exhibiting this piece, what would you call it?'

He stopped working for a couple of beats, thinking.

'Resting,' he said. And there it was, that heaviness in the mouth, lips parted for breath; the lower lip that you could bite.

'I'm cutting my nails,' said Sue, 'he wants them for the fingers. I don't know where this is going to end. He's persuaded Terry to do another alligator.' There Terry was, getting the claws fitted to the scaly monster that dominated half the room.

'What I'd like,' said Terry, 'is for the lads on the gardens to make a place for it outside, have it lurking in the undergrowth.'

'With water-lillies and bulrushes?' I asked him getting into the swing of his fantasy.

'That's it,' he said, delighted to have pulled me in, 'just outside my pad window so I can keep an eye on it.'

Neil turned to us, suddenly loquacious. 'I was going to start with the skull, on the gorilla, and then build up the sinew and the muscle, but I can't find the right pictures to do it from. Lady in the library found me the diagrams for the skull. I'll do another I think and keep this one as a skull. It'll not take long, five or six days. I'll do a proper head. One of the guys on the wing, a ginger guy, he's growing his beard for me. Down to here it is already. I've said I'll buy it off him for a packet of biscuits. Thought I'd stick it on see? Start at the crest of the bone and let it fall down the sides of his head.' I'd never heard him say more than two words before.

'You're going to do what?' said Terry.

'Carl,' Neil told him,' gonna let me have his beard.'

'It'll be like an orang-utan.'

'Well, I could do an orang-utan next.'

Sue had gone quiet, suddenly lost in thought.

'If we could persuade the Prison Service,' she said, 'to send us a lot of ginger haired prisoners we could do life size ones. We could have a what-do-you-call-it, a troupe.' No-one speaks.

'Did I tell you,' she said, oblivious, 'that the guys in the blacksmith shop say they'll make a cage for him when he's finished?'

Neil and Terry looked at her and then exchanged worried looks. 'It's not, you know, actually alive Sue,' said Terry.

'I know it's not bloody alive,' she snapped at him. But they knew that they'd caught her in something and they smiled.

Neil and Terry were smiling, that was quite something. It would be easy to think of art as therapy. After all, the question, 'What good does it do?' is a reasonable one. Does it stop them reoffending? These were not questions that Sue had much time for.

'How the bloody hell should I know? Not much bothered. Don't think about it.' And hearing that was always a relief. I was always left a bit tongue-tied when someone asked me about that sort of thing. Left to myself I would never think about it either. I never had much idea about what good, or bad for that matter, I might be doing.

Just reflect for a moment: how could writing a poem, or knowing what Hume thought, or making a sculpture put you off armed robbery or heroin. It might make you happy but how on earth can it make you good? Good might be a bit ambitious; could Shakespeare make you good; more likely to make you bad. Even a humbler target like, say, being law-abiding seems at least unlikely. Actually it seems entirely unlikely. The things that Sue and I do might provide a distraction, fill up the time that might otherwise be filled with crime. As a straw to clutch at this is really not up to much.

Weighing everything that we do in Education in terms of reform is a part of the notion that in prison everyone we taught was a criminal, a demon, a breed apart, a sub-species which spent all of its life in criminality, a tribe dedicated to evil with a discreet set of values alien to civilised life.

My guess is that most criminals are not criminals most of the time. Most of the criminals, no, most of the men I met who happened to be in prison were somebody's son, lover, husband, father; they were football supporters, stamp collectors, theatregoers and so on and on. They only spent a tiny fraction of their time being criminals. Drugs and mental illness distort this claim, of course and Art and Philosophy are not going to turn back those tides.

So, why not give Sue and me the sack? Art and Philosophy and Literature and all the rest of the fluffy stuff is what all of us do when we are at our best, when we are most distinctively human. I think that people like Sue and I give our students the chance to be more human. The same reason, then, that anybody at all, anywhere does that fluffy thing. Just think about it: who would you like to spend time with a fluffy person or a non-fluffy person. There you are in the pub, or on A Wing, and some bore is going on about cars or football and over there someone is telling jokes about Shakespeare and Jean-Paul Sartre, what do you do, who would you prefer to spend your evening with?

18

Marx, Rousseau and Peter Pan

Patrick and Wesley were both doing 15 years for armed robbery. It sounds terrible and, of course, when you think of what it entails, it is. But armed robbers brought with them a whiff of another world, a world where dreadful, deadly goings-on were smiled at, spoken of with a rough matter of fact acceptance. As full of unresolved contradictions as the gangster films where you want the villains to get away. Wesley would claim that, 'I dreaded having an ordinary life, I wanted a bit of, you know, adventure.' But as we went along he emerged as a family man, someone who had run a business, gone to the theatre, liked surrealism and cooking and basketball. He was only about five per cent an adventurer.

Patrick, though, Patrick would break your heart. He was obviously a big tough sort of a guy but there was something refined about him. He was Irish and he was Caribbean, an African and a Celt. He was the one who organized Black History Month and he was the one who could tell you about Irish history. I never really knew what was going on with Patrick but we were always on good terms. When he began coming to my classes he was already half way into a Philosophy degree with the OU and he was unsmilingly serious about it, one of those students who made life easy. For a start there was no messing about; Philosophy, he made it clear, was what we were there for. I made the awkward discovery that I was one of the disruptive influences in the room that it could well be me who liked a bit of a diversion, a bit of a joke and a doss. He and Wesley were not above telling me off, not above offering guidance to some of the other guys about the possible consequences of poor behaviour.

More often than not Patrick would wear a Parachute Regiment T-shirt. The thing he regretted about being caught wasn't the 16 year sentence.

'Fair enough,' he told me, it was being dismissed from the army. He got into rivalries in the gym, not quite friendly rivalries, with a couple of the gym officers who had been in the Marines. Some things transcended jail. But beyond all this Patrick was good at Philosophy, really good, in that obsessive way that sometimes occurs. Patrick had found something that was saving his sense of himself and marking him out as special and individual.

When we got into Philosophy of Mind I could let him take over and he would run us through all that complicated stuff, that I only half understood, about other minds and the Chinese Box argument. Not all of the class kept up with this. To be honest some of them were a bit lost. I could confess to my own difficulties and tell them that the problem of consciousness was actually real cutting-edge stuff that everyone was struggling with and we would sit there nodding wisely at each other. They were pleased to know that Patrick was into all this obscure, elitist stuff.

'People like us, see, we're not useless.' It created an odd atmosphere. It wasn't just Patrick who had this effect, over the years there had usually been someone like this in the room. Charles could do it and Cal, Ahmed, Jay and Luke. I would get odd looks: 'See, clever bugger, we're not the ignorant bastards you took us for.'

I usually avoided going up onto the wings, the residential parts of the prison. It was all too depressing and invited me to think of my students as prisoners. Patrick was on the Lifer Wing. I let myself in through the iron gate and the solid wooden door, that sealed off the wing, locked them behind me and checked in with the officers.

'Is it okay to see Patrick?'

They just waved me through: 'Yeah, if you like. Second landing,' and they told me the number. I had not thought that they would leave me to find my own way and for the first time ever I felt the claustrophobic sense of nervousness edging into fear. It was a forceful reminder of how much I relied on, and took for granted, the presence of the officers. It was association and there were too many bodies and too many looks in my direction. I asked someone where Patrick was and he must have picked out my voice because, all at once, there he was, embarrassed, flustered.

'What you doin' here?'

'Your UCAS forms.'

'Come on, come on.' And he hustled me into his pad.

The cells were tiny: bed, table, chair, toilet, sink and for Patrick there were books and papers and a couple of photos. Everything was starkly tidy, blankets folded square. 'Get you a coffee?' he had a tiny jar with just a dusting left in it.

'Yes please,' I said as I knew I must. Patrick was offering me what he had to offer and it was important that I took it. We sat on the bed drinking black coffee out of blue plastic mugs and got through the business in no time.

'You want to see my deps?'

'What?'

'Stuff from my trial.'

'Yes, alright then.'

He pulled a big polythene bag from under the bed and grinned.

'Got all the photos.'

'How do you mean?'

'My photos.'

He had, in a sequence of stills, the CCTV footage of the bank robbery. There he was in the bank, caught nicely, big gun in one hand and a bag of money in the other, dreads whirling round as he turned, over his shoulder the white, startled face of a woman. A big black gunman with dreadlocks; I couldn't help wondering.

'That's your idea of a disguise is it?' I said, pointing at the sunglasses.

'Yeah, yeah, alright. When I got home people were ringing me up saying: "Hey Pat, just saw you on the news."'

We sat there in his cell, seven years into his 16 year sentence. As soon as Wesley arrived in the prison Patrick brought him to class. Wesley was doing Sociology with the OU. A couple of months later they brought Spud who was doing OU Music. The room seemed very full. Wesley was conscious of his history in a way which completely escaped Patrick. Whereas Patrick accepted racism as an inevitable and trivial aspect of life Wesley was having none of it. He brought home to me how powerful a force slavery remained in defining how we live now. For Wesley what had happened in the eighteenth century was still a living, raw memory. I would always try to point out that the plight of the English working-class then and later was no better than slavery and he would always have none of it.

The room divided between my Marxism, Wesley's Marxism too for that matter, and the dogged right wing patriotism which drove Patrick. People started to sit in groups again; there were hard stares across the Formica tables. Marxists and Tories, we would take strong positions which would collapse into absurd faction fighting between Stalinists and Trots, Anarchists and Liberals.

Glenn, from Probation, would use Patrick and Wesley to give talks to local schoolchildren about the dreadfulness not just of prison but of being involved in crime at all. I'm not sure how sincere they were: there was Wesley's desire for the life of adventure, Patrick's cheerful stoicism. Patrick was reduced to panic, maybe for the first time in his life, when he was cast in the lead in a play. It wasn't a big affair, just a short piece about crime and prison and so on.

'My arse went. I was terrified. Still am every time we do it.' He did it though, and Glenn took him and the rest out to schools and sometimes some of the local kids came into the prison.

One of the other guys, Harry, was a bit worried that one girl was impervious to it all. 'Hard faced little cow. Then, I happened to mention that I'd never had a McDonald's. She couldn't believe it. "Why not?" Didn't have McDonald's love, not when I came into prison. McDonald's, the one thing that got through. Funny really.'

When Patrick was due for his Cat-D Glenn and I had the bright idea that he could commute to a university. I was a bit shocked that people turned him down and at one point I had a bit of a row with an admissions tutor on the phone. Patrick was sitting in the office with me; he looked embarrassed. 'Alan,' he said, 'don't you think we're being a bit cheeky.' I couldn't believe it, he was standing there, fumbling and blushing. I was outraged.

'What?' I said, 'Me, cheeky? Don't you think it was a bit fucking cheeky robbing banks at gunpoint?'

He looked shocked, offended and it dawned on me that he hadn't thought it a particularly wrong thing to do.

Afterwards, when I had thought about it, I was a bit shocked myself to realise that he thought that he wasn't up to university, that it was a frightening thing and that, in a very depressing way, he wasn't worthy. It made me remember how I had felt in 1966 when I got the letter saying that, yes, I could come to the university and here's a reading list and, yes, we look forward to seeing you. I was a scruffy kid from the back streets of Sheffield. When I got to York I checked that my name was up there on the lists on the notice board and I went back a few times; it was still there, no mistakes, no delusion.

There had been a similar performance a year or so before with Bernard. When I first broached the subject of university he said: 'You talk through your arse sometimes Boss.' After five years in prison I could forgive him the odd slip into pessimism. 'Who's going to have me? Go on, who? They won't even let me out for a day, just one day, I couldn't even go for an interview. Anyway how would you like it if your daughter was on the same course as an armed robber this October?'

All six of his UCAS choices turned him down and it was a bit of a struggle to keep him working on his A-Level courses. Sometimes it felt as though the whole Education Department had been drawn into project Bernard as we all talk-talk-talked to him, endlessly, about keeping going, being optimistic, staying out of trouble, doing the reading, writing the letters, filling in the forms. Bernard was still only 23-years-old and prison had kept him much younger than that. He hated prison and drove himself and everyone else crazy because of this so that there was no-one in the place who had not at times felt the urgent desire to horsewhip him. He was, though, charming and intelligent, you could bring him home for tea without a single qualm.

One Thursday we got the exam results and I went to the computer room, where he was working away, and sat down with him.

'With your grades we ought really to get you into the clearing system.'

'You reckon it will do any good?'

I knew that he had a plan; he told me about it endlessly.

'If I can get a place at the University of X I can live with my auntie. She'll look after me, make me behave. I can get a part-time job. I know where I can be a model, you know for Art College, in the nude. Really well paid it is.' As plans went this was not bad because Bernard had a physique that only the stark prison regime and endless gym can give. 'You'll have to be careful about erections,' I told him. 'You haven't seen a girl for five years and you know what art students are like.'

He sat with me in the office and I started telephoning. All the great bulk of him, sitting round shouldered, chin down, both hands pressed tightly between his thighs, like a little lost kid. 'I'm calling from Her Majesty's Prison,' I said down the phone.

'Oh no,' Bernard hissed at me, 'don't say that. Don't tell them that.'

We had to wait a little while for someone who could make a decision. Just long enough for Bernard to start moaning about how he should have got better grades and for me to snap at him. When they rang back I told them that he would be free at the end of August.

'They say you can start on the 25th of September,' I told him, 'will that do for you?'

He pursed his lips, sucked in his cheeks and went big eyed.

'He says, yes that'll be fine and thank you very much.'

I put the phone down and we sat and looked at each other for a moment. Then he said, 'I'm scared you know Boss. I'm really scared.'

It was probably to do with Patrick's recruiting efforts but the Philosophy Class filled up with men who were doing long sentences for some quite violent things. I never asked but there were always stories being told about adventures and chases, plots and shootouts, cars, women, schemes. They made it all seem rather attractive in the way that Robert Louis Stevenson persuaded me to like Long John Silver.

I was never too keen on going away for the holidays, it always seemed a bit churlish telling guys who've been locked up for a decade that you're off to France for three weeks. 'I don't like holidays much, not my sort of thing,' I told them. But they shook my hand, 'Have a good one Al.' How could I tell them about the food and the wine? 'Fill your boots mate.' I was always struck by the robust, in your face optimism that got them through, the whistling in the dark.

When I got back from holiday I sometimes had the impression that there were things that they had saved up for me. I'd been away for a good long break, and I'd forgotten just how things can be. Of course, they were pleased to see me and, of course, I had the usual mixed feelings about them. All that time away, all the stuff we'd done in France and there they were, there they still are, some of them with huge sentences, just doing it and doing it. Yes, I know, I know all the arguments about sentencing and justice and what people might or might not deserve but as far as my philosophers are concerned I don't give a bugger about any of that.

Before I went off I had persuaded my university colleague, Lawrence, to take the class for a few weeks. I'm not too keen about leaving them with Laurence. He's the sort of bloke who really does know what he's talking about and I expected that the call my bluff school of coarse Philosophy that I go in for would be sadly exposed. I knew that, too, there were some quite handy characters in the group but Wesley and Patrick had always exerted a calming influence and Ronny from New York was a force for good, at least when he was being philosophical. One of the guys, Jerome, could have some difficult moments but Patrick said that they had counselled him up on the wing about his conduct in class and they promised to look after Lawrence. When I got back it was clear that he had made an impression.

'That Lawrence bloke, he gets really excited doesn't he?' Patrick said 'We had to keep him in order.'

'Well,' I said, 'he's really into it.'

'He wanted to smoke; we stopped him. Then he wanted to smoke out of the window. I said no, mate, no you can't do that. If you can smoke we can smoke.'

'Yeah,' said Richard, 'He was really pissed off.'

'You couldn't get away with anything with him, though,' said Patrick, 'he really, like, pinned you down.

That's one thing I've learned in Philosophy, you really have to get it straight about what words mean. There was this guy on the wing the other day going on about 'feminine' and I didn't understand him. So I was going, 'what do you mean, what do you mean?' and eventually I got it out of him that he really wanted to talk about vulnerability. I could have hugged him. But he was caught up in something else.

'Vulnerability,' he said, as if it had just occurred to him. There was a pause, as if he were making up his mind to trust us. 'I'll tell you something. I was on the wing, just going past the showers and just out the corner of my eye I saw this guy. Fucking hell, he had the biggest dick you've ever seen. I've not told anybody this, I mean, how can you? People would be going round saying that I was the sort that went round looking at people's dicks.' I had planned to talk about Rousseau. 'I'm telling you it hung half way down his leg.'

'Bet he faints when he gets an erection,' said Jack.

'I didn't like it,' said Patrick, 'It made me feel vulnerable. What's that about then? Why should I feel like that?'

And that's how we spent the morning talking about masculinity, power, vulnerability.

'There's a guy on our wing,' said Richard, 'and he stands like a puff. You know hand on his hip and all that and he's really getting badly misunderstood. He's straight. I had to explain it to him. I've been teaching him how to stand.'

I can just imagine it, Richard giving classes in deportment during association. They do, they save it up for me.

When I got back to the university Lawrence came to see me. He had a slightly different tale to tell.

'You fucker,' he said.

'Yes, thanks for asking; I've had a nice holiday.'

'You fucker, you never told me about that Jerome did you?'

'I did.'

'You never said he was fucking barmy.'

'Jerome's alright.'

'Alright? All fucking right? He tried to kill little Walter. Seven officers, seven, took seven of them to get him out.'

I couldn't help but laugh, in fact I thought it was hysterical. Later on, though, I had a little go at the guys about it all. They smiled. 'Seven?' they said, 'nah, it was never seven.'

'Anyway,' I said, pleased to be back, 'you're well then are you?'

'Yeah,' said Wesley, 'I'm all right now.'

'He's been sulking,' said Patrick

'I always sulk when I'm ill. I've just been lying there sweating. Had to change the mattress, it was soaked. Anyway, I don't care about all that, I got an unconditional offer from UCAS'

Patrick and Spud had got Wesley back into the OU. He'd had a go at it some years before but the two of them had got him sparked up again. We had spent quite a bit of time in the computer room putting together his personal statement for UCAS. He wasn't quite able to work out what to say that would recommend him and I think that he was a little bit surprised when I insisted that we mention all the reading that he did, his interest in slavery and Black History and especially his liking for opera. I tried to get out of him why he liked opera, where all of that had come from. But, he couldn't for the life of him work it out.

'Just like it, always have done, even when I was a kid.' And he told me about spending his money on the Royal Opera House and Glyndbourne while his mates were out doing God knows what. It hadn't been difficult to make him sound terrific.

'Unconditional? You sure that's what it says?'

I got the big smile, all teeth and moustache, the little modest shake of the head.

'Yeah, they really want me. Just next to where I live it is. Course I'll have to get parole or D Cat or something. Can't just do it can I?'

'Just defer it for a bit then,' I said.

'Yeah,' he said.

'That's not right is it?' said Patrick. 'I've got exams to pass. Why are they just letting him in?'

'Quality my son,' said Wesley.

'Is your wife pleased?' I asked him.

'Yeah she's well chuffed mate. She really looks after me. She gets on the phone to everybody telling them what a blinder I am. When I was ill just now, Patrick's wife phoned her to tell her and she was onto the prison straightaway worrying about my health. She gets on the phone to the universities. Does everything.'

'She sounds terrific. What's she doing married to a tosser like you for?'

'I don't know mate. I don't, really I don't.' He had to turn away, head down looking sheepish. As sheepish as a giant can look.

'Patrick's Missis, she's the same.'

'Every time she sees me now,' said Patrick, 'every visit, I get a telling off about looking after myself. You can't imagine the trouble I'm in at the moment.

'What trouble?' I had a moment of panic, fearing the worst; you never know in prison.

'She's worrying that I've lost weight.' He gave a huge biceps a quick flex, checked himself out.

'Well, I think you might have,' I said, deciding not to flex anything back at him.

'I gave up my gym so I could come to English Classes.'

'Yeah,' said Wesley, 'you're starting to look a bit what do you call it, a bit elfin.'

'Carry on like this Patrick,' I told him, 'and you could be cast as the first black Peter Pan.

I get a bad look from under the dreads: 'Could be, could well be. I do some acting you know.'

Yes, I know.'

'For the youth project.'

'You said.'

'I'm the lead I am.'

'You have mentioned it,' I say.

'Once or twice,' said Wesley.

'Brilliant I am. We do it for schoolkids. We do the play and then there's question and answer. There was this girl, she'd be about 15, black and red hair, piercings; like something from *Lord Of The Flies* she was. Had her in tears, made her realise. Bit on the weird side really. Anyway, we try to put them off crime and all this,' waving his hand at the prison.

'And you're good are you?'

'Brilliant,' he said and laughed. 'I'll tell you what, nine years ago, when I'd just been sentenced I could never have dreamed that things would have turned out like this. I just sat there in the cell head in my hands, that's it, I thought, my life's over.'

Then Patrick had an offer. Someone had picked up on his OU modules, his O-Levels, his A-Levels, all the training in the Paras. And a couple of weeks after that the prison granted him a day's licence so that he could visit the university that had made him the offer. Glenn, from Probation, drove him. 'Total sensory overload,' said Patrick. 'We had to drive dead slow; I couldn't cope with it at first. We stopped and had breakfast. I had toast.'

'You had what?' said Wesley. 'Everything to pick from and you had toast?'

'I've missed toast. Can't get toast in prison. Not real toast.'

There's that familiar feeling of delight and sorrow when someone like Patrick leaves. Someone like Patrick who has done the reading, learned to write the essays, opened himself up to being judged, graded, commented upon. The sorts of things that are difficult for any adult student but which, in the context of prison, can seem like an assault on a man's identity.

'Yes,' he says, 'they want me settled into D cat before the university term starts. I reckon they must have had a special board just for me.' He looks amazed. I was a bit amazed myself at the way that everyone, Governors, Probation, Education Managers, the University had got this absolutely right and everything had fallen into place.

'Yeah go on,' said Wesley, 'fuck off. We're all sick of the fucking sight of you anyway.' It made me realise that Patrick's leaving would be a blow for him. It was a blow for me too; for months now I'd been able to persuade Patrick to explain to the guys, explain to me as well come to that, about Isaiah Berlin or other minds or the poverty of common sense. One morning, for example, we had been talking about John Rawls and what sort of a society you would want to live in. Patrick had no doubt that a Thatcherite society, a meritocracy contained within a hierarchy, would be just the job.

'What if you were at the bottom?' Max asked.

'You'd deserve to be,' said Patrick and Max was on him in a flash, gave him a good bashing with his OU Social Sciences, telling him just how society conspires to keep the lower classes low. Then, out of the blue, from Wesley of all people, we got a wistful description of what an Anarchist Utopia would be like, a society where there would be equality, justice, no money. It seduced Max and let Patrick off the hook so that he could talk now about how the inevitability of corruption and social mobility making static utopias impossible to sustain.

It seemed a bit hard that Patrick should use his last lesson to give Wesley such a comprehensive working over. But, then, Wesley struck back and Patrick had to concede that justice involved establishing some sort of equilibrium between talent and need. Max was still dogging away at him in that quiet, reasonable way that he had and so Patrick created a diversion. He insisted that every member of the group gave an opinion. He went round the room, imposing, very Thatcherite, very authoritarian, an opinion poll. He even made Regis say something. Regis was a French speaker and came to Philosophy because it had the best standard of spoken English he could listen to in the prison.

'Oi, don't look away, come on, what do you think?'

And Regis had to say something with all eyes on him.

All I'd done that morning was mark the register. And that's another thing; the register, the roll-check for the officers, the form that ensures that the guys get paid, I have to get it all spot on, now that I have created a monster.

The Education Department were looking for a new orderly and I recommended Marlon. He got the job and was delighted. Came to shake my hand. The next time that he saw me he gave me a talking to about doing the paperwork properly and not messing him about. He wagged his finger, 'Don't give me no trouble.' It made the office staff smile.

At the end of the lesson we stood in the corridor and said our goodbyes to Patrick. Then he and Wesley stepped back into the room, 'We'd like to see you, on your own.' They weren't smiling. Wesley shut the door and we sat down.

Patrick looked embarrassed: 'Look Al I've learned a lot here,' he paused, 'but…'

Wesley, impatient with the pussyfooting, said: 'Listen, you want to start being more careful,' and out of the blue I was getting a bollocking. They'd been watching me, I'd done a couple of stupid things and they thought that I needed to remember about being safe in the prison.

'You sound just like Security,' I said, trying to make a joke. But they were not having it, it was not a joke.

'Listen Al, there are some right evil bastards in prison. Security are only trying to keep you safe.' Now he was wagging his finger.

Patrick lasted two weeks at the university and then he did something silly, lost his Cat-D and was back in a Cat-B prison.

'What can you do?' said Spud, 'he's fucked up. It happens.'

After the first shock, and I think that I was the only one who was shocked, Glen in particular was very stoical, I didn't feel even a bit disappointed and I certainly didn't blame him. We had always got on. I was as foreign to him as he was to me but we could sit and listen to each other all day.

Wesley was offered a place in a Cat-D somewhere freezing and northern where there was a farm. Spud and I were delighted to think of him, an urbane elegant black man, looking after the sheep and pigs in East Coast blizzards and dreaming about Puccini.

About a year later I was asked to write a reference for Wesley for one of the northern universities; after that, I don't know.

19

Poker, Pool and John Coltrane

One day I was limping down the corridor and Liz, Yoga Liz the guys called her, stopped me and said: 'What's the matter with you?' in the accusing way that she had.

'It's my knee.'

'Put your thumbs in your belly button.'

'What?'

'Now, look. See where your fingers are? That's where your muscle is. It goes right down into your leg. You need to massage it; it's clearly not happy.'

She had a bit of a reputation for instant, rather painful cures, sticking her thumbs into people, so that the men preferred not to mention their ailments for fear of being brutalised.

'A lot of people who aren't as wimpy as you come to Yoga Classes,' she told me.

'Not just the lads.' She did lunchtime classes for staff.

Jeff, the officer on duty in Education today, nodded.

'A lot of the officers did yoga at my last prison,' he said. 'Can be seen as a bit of a girly thing but it's not, it's a really useful thing.' Jeff didn't look even a little bit girly. 'In fact, last night I was talking to one of the lads up on the wing; he's going to go to Liz's class this afternoon.' He made it sound as though the guy didn't have much choice.

But, Liz was smiling.

'There have been some men who come to the class and they just sit there, don't do a thing. They just want the quiet and the calmness. One little bit of calmness can infect a lot of people.' She stood straight and touched her shoulders. 'That's where the anger is, in the chest and shoulders. Once they can open up there, physically, then that makes the difference. When Eddy started with me, he was all tensed up. You look now at the way he holds himself.'

'Eddy?'

'Oh yes, Eddy comes to yoga. You ask him about it.'

'Didn't know you did yoga,' I said to Eddy at our next Philosophy Class and he surprised me with his enthusiasm

'Go to the classes? Sure I do. I do it in my pad at night now when things have quietened down. That's the best time. The breathing and the postures. Every morning: Salutation to the Sun.'

'Doesn't all that spiritual stuff get you down a bit?'

'Not at all.'

'All that "I am at one with the universe nonsense".'

'It's no nonsense, Alan.'

'Oh come on.'

'Come on my arse.'

'Makes a difference does it?'

'Listen, when was the last time I lost at pool up on the wing?'

'What?'

'I'll tell you. I never lose at pool, not now, and it's a major part of my income.'

'What are you talking about?'

'I pick up the cue and I put myself in that place, you know?' he makes a flowing, balletic movement with his hands, doing the breathing.

'And I'm saying to myself: "I am at one with the cue; I am at one with the baize."' He gave me the dreadful, vulpine smile. 'I never lose. I can concentrate and the other tossers are no fuckin' where. I stopped for a while and my performance collapsed. My game went to pieces. No concentration. If I do it right, follow the path, you know, I just blow people away.'

Winning the yoga way could be dangerous. Not for Eddy, of course, his talents went beyond yoga and pool. When Neil, a couple of years later, found that he could not lose at poker it was a different story. Not that Neil was by any means a pushover but it did occur to him that storm clouds were brewing.

'It's the yoga, Alan.'

'Yes, I've heard this before.'

'I can just put my mind to things. I can count the cards, I can remember who did what. You just breathe and you're in the zone. The other guys who play, you know what they're like, they gamble, they take chances. I don't. I know what's going to happen because I know what's already happened.'

'I am at one with the cards,' I said.

'What?'

'Never mind.'

'Anyway, I've started losing on purpose. I always come out ahead but I make sure to have ups and downs. I had all the burn on the landing, I had a chocolate mountain, IOUs. It was starting to get nasty. People were making me roll my sleeves up to deal. They were looking at the cards for marks and pinpricks. Started accusing me of cheating.'

'Well you are cheating.'

'No mate, it's spiritual.'

In Liz's room it obviously is. Just before the Friday afternoon class, Matthew told me: 'It ought to be compulsory—if you didn't do yoga in jail you should get nicked.'

'He's right,' said Rick. 'In prison, little things are big things. It's a demagnifier. It's not bendy back yoga. Could never do that, this just takes the week away. It supplements gym. I don't want to get big and lumpy.'

'Yeah,' said Len, 'do it before gym and it loosens your bones.'

The desks and chairs were stacked away and the nine men were lying on their blue mats looking up at Liz, waiting to begin.

'Just have a wriggle,' she said. 'Wriggling is really good. Wriggle when you're tense.'

'If I have a good wriggle in bed tonight,' someone asked, 'will it help me sleep?'

'Of course it will,' Liz said, gently. 'Just you wriggle all that tension away.'

She got them into the breathing exercises and the class was under way. They were absolutely serious, absolutely alone, taken for once out of the huge collectivity of the prison.

'Breathing,' she told them, 'makes time and space for yourself.' And lets you win at poker, I thought to myself.

Outside the room a gate banged, footsteps clipped along in the stark echoing corridor; we could hear keys jangling and the big, echoing voices that filled the prison. The silence the men had made pierced the noise.

At the end of the afternoon there was an odd feeling of surprise in the air. 'Did you notice that?' Liz asked.

Don looked a bit detached: 'It takes you to places where you can't hear all the rubbish,' he said. 'Charges you up.'

One lunch time Yoga Liz asked me if I'd met Spud yet. She'd been up on the wing and had heard him practising. 'Marvellous,' she said, 'absolutely marvellous. You know how big and echoey it is. He's in his cell, door open, but you can't work out where it's coming from at first and this sound just fills the wing. There's music everywhere. And nobody complains because it's proper stuff, not the usual damned racket.'

It wasn't long before he had found his way into Philosophy with Patrick and Wesley. He stood in the doorway a bit hesitant, dreads piled up on his head and round cherubic face. Then he started an argument with Wesley about Mind Body Dualism.

'Have you done this before?' I asked him.

'OU,' he said, 'doing Music and Philosophy.'

'Yes', Liz told me. 'Saxophone. Must be a bit difficult for the guys next door.'

He laughed, shook his head, 'No, no it's not. They love it. I'm good I am. I'm not bragging, I'm really not. It's all I've done for ten years and I can really do it. I've got all sorts of things worked out. Guys I used to play with, when I was just a honker, they come in on visits and they're trying to find out stuff I'm doing. Nothing, I tell them nothing, give nothing away. One day I'm gonna make them astonished. That's what they're doing, trying to steal my shit. I've been practising for ten years Al and when I get out I'm gonna blow them away.'

But then, next lesson, Spud didn't show up.

'Where's Spud?' I asked.

Wesley said that he was having a bit of a crisis and that he'd volunteered himself to go onto Seg, solitary. I was astonished: 'What? What for?'

'It's difficult Al, sometimes it's difficult.' And I knew that it was, especially for men who came to us from a higher category prison where they might have been for years in one particular regime. The degree of change that they experienced was a huge test.

At break Spud came in looking sheepish and we all laughed at him and made some smart remarks about what a prick he was and made him smile.

'I feel such a fool,' he said. 'You know, I'm playing my horn, playing for say an hour or so and I step outside my pad and it's like that, what do you call it, catharsis, and I want to talk to somebody about what I'm doing and there isn't anybody. It doesn't happen and I brood a bit and that's it, fuck the lot of you I'm goin' to the Seg, to be on my own. So I get all packed up, fuck everybody, and then the officers start being nice to me. I got as far as the gate and then I failed. What were they being nice to me for, persuading me to stay on the wing? "Are you sure about this Spud?" All nice and concerned, making my courage fail. I was weak. Everybody knows I was weak; all my soldier credit gone.'

But, he got through it and his OU degree took him over. When we spent a few weeks talking about Aesthetics he brought in some Coltrane, *Romanian Suicide Song,* and got a huge range of reaction, a bit of a row really.

'There's no fuckin' suicide in it.'

'Well, it's mournful.'

'My arse it's mournful, it's glamorous.'

'It's both,' Spud said, 'It's Coltrane.' And then he got us into the Intentionalist Fallacy, made us focus on where it was that a work of art existed and what kinds of things might we say about meaning and how meaning only seems to be definite and that saying what something means never closes the question of its meaning. He was pretty good.

A few weeks ago, in the middle of John Locke, Sue, the Education Manager, put her head round the door, 'Can I have Spud?'

'What, what?' said Spud, 'Has it come?'

He got back a few minutes later with a big cardboard box. The guys made him unwrap it and we had a brief Christmas moment with Spud looking delighted and silly and then embarrassed when he had to explain why the OU had sent him a keyboard. It was a small, black plastic keyboard as basic as you can get and he was knocked out.

In pre-keyboard days we had conversations about Mingus and Coltrane. But now, post-keyboard, it wasn't just jazz, it was Beethoven, Chopin, Schubert.

'I can write it down. You know like in a note book. Like when Mozart or somebody went for a walk and they got a tune, an idea, they could write it down and then when they got home they played what they wrote and it worked. I can do that. I can.'

I asked about his OU tutor, if he was any good?

'Good? Good? He's pukka. He's giving me confidence. When I played I used to think, "Am I just a honker?" But he plays chords and I just recognise them and he tells me my ears are really good. I'm learning the rules and I'm really getting on top, you know, in improvisation. He's given me this to learn; we're going to play it together. It's beautiful.' It's an odd word to hear in the prison. He showed me the sheets of music: Elgar Opus 12 *Salut d'Amour*.

I'm still not sure what happened after that. He started to miss his classes and when I asked in the office Sue told me that he was struggling to write his essays for the OU. I tried to get him to come and see me about it but that just put a stop to his coming to any classes at all.

Studying in prison is a fragile activity and when there is a hint of failure in the air then sometimes the reaction is to shut down completely. There is, for some men, just too much to lose. The pressure of being in prison, of living that life, for years-and-years, is easy to underestimate. The first duty is a duty of self-defence.

I still saw Spud from time to time and he was still playing. He kept on with Liz and I think that the yoga got him through some bad moments. He more than held his own but I think that he was a bit too sensitive to be locked up. He got a job in the kitchens, moved on to his Cat-D and, I presume to release on licence. I guess that he made the right move. There were times when I just had to keep my mouth shut. It was easy to get carried away with all the good educational ideas: 'Why don't you do this? Why don't you do that?' I wasn't the one living in the prison regime.

20

They Love a Bad Boy

It began with Aristotle. The lovely common sense of Virtue Theory was such a relief after Plato. The chaps were much taken with the notion that things like reasonable good looks, a degree of wealth could be thought of as virtues. My mistake was to suggest that truth-telling and keeping your promises would also tend towards making someone's life a success.

'Not with women though,' said Adrian.

Faces lit up in agreement, sideways glances eyes wide with shock at the very idea of any kind of straight dealing where women were concerned. They were patient with me and tried hard, as might a deluded child, to explain the realities. The thing that hit me the hardest was that there was world-wide consensus. 'They don't know what truth is,' an American view, 'I was in this woman's bed an' she was phoning up her man in jail tellin' him she love him.'

There was knowing laughter; they weren't having any of my none-sense.

'That's what they're like Al, honest it is.'

'But you can't go around lying to people,' I was getting a bit desperate, 'If somebody calls you a liar, how do you feel about that?'

Adrian stepped in with a West African perspective.

'It's a good thing for you, good for your eudaimonia, if women think you're a liar.' That's the thanks you get from Philosophy students, a good rogering with something Greek and slippery.

'Women expect you to lie to them, so you lie to them.'

'What even if you don't need to?'

'But of course,' He was beaming, 'it's what you have to do.'

I was struggling to grasp his point 'So, you think they'd be hurt if you didn't lie, didn't make the effort?'

He leaned forward, suddenly very serious, even wagged his finger to make sure I learned the lesson: 'Alan, they love a bad boy. Let me tell you, all of them, they love a bad boy. So, you lie to them and you let them know it, make sure that they know that you're a liar.'

Then Keith, with an English point of view this time, started on me, 'Tell them anything man.'

Then Eddy from Scotland. 'It's as if they want to be deceived, conspire at their own downfall,' he said. Then, he gave me a bit of my own back. 'Reality is after all a very fragile construct that might have little to do with the external world. If there is such a thing as the external world. After all it might just be our way of talking about things. Whatever things might be.' Things had turned nasty. I thought about pressing the alarm button. What would I say though when the officers burst in, 'These bastards are carrying offensive concepts.'?

'Now let me tell you,' Oliver had a big smile on his face, sheepish and delighted. He had been around a bit: Africa, Europe, Russia. 'My wife, she caught me with another girl,' he chuckled to himself, full of good humour, as he remembered, 'She looked out of the window of the flat where we were living.'

'Where was that?'

'Moscow, I was at the University of Moscow, and I was on the street kissing this girl. When I got in my wife started to accuse me, so I just denied it. "No, not me. I never did that." I deny, deny, deny. "You never saw any such a thing."'

'See what I mean,' said Eddy, 'claiming to know something is claiming that you have good reason to believe it. It's just discourse.' Well, that was me finished.

Oliver went on: 'I said to her, "It must have been somebody else. You just made a mistake."'

'What?' I didn't often shout, 'how many giant, black, Nigerians lived in your part of Moscow?'

He smiled, 'It doesn't matter, nothing makes any difference as long as you lie and lie and lie. And then, when you just keep talking, she starts to say to herself, "Did I see this thing, perhaps I didn't?" and all she knows is what you tell her.'

'See what I mean,' said Eddie.

'What about,' and this is what they had reduced me to, 'what about your mother, or your daughter?'

Oliver stared at me, his face, for a moment, filled with doubt and then with a big, puzzled frown he said: 'When women have babies, what happens?'

'You what?' Was he taking the piss? No, he was serious. I looked round the room, as they all were doing.

'How big does it get?' Oliver wanted to know.

'Well,' I was floundering, 'the head's got to come out. So it's got to be, you know, big.'

'Yeah,' said Austin, 'and the shoulders. See, what happens is this...' and he took us through the whole business: things dilating, contractions, breathing, stitches, everything. There was deathly silence.

'How'd you know all that then?' said Oliver.

'I was there when all my kids were born.'

'How many you got?'

'Ten.'

Quite naturally I think, we drifted, away from all the frightening reality into talking about happiness and were pleased with the more worldly commonsense views of Aristotle than the arcane psychological calculations that Bentham invited us to make. It seemed to be a good idea to bring Schoepenhauer out for a dusting and, of course, while they liked the notion that swallowing a toad for breakfast would make the rest of the day seem relatively OK, they couldn't help but feel that he must have been a miserable bastard and anyway where would they find a toad a day in the nick. But then there was the Will to Life.

'I've got that,' said Nathan, smiling sheepishly. The Will to Life, according to Schopenhauer, is the blind, unconscious, irresistible will to reproduce. 'I've got five kids. I was there for all of them when they were born,' he touched his eyes with his fingertips, 'and I was just in tears. When I met my girl she wouldn't have nothing to do with me. She had me sussed. It went on for months man, she wouldn't let me touch her. So I knew, didn't I, that she wasn't a slag. Anyway, now we've got an eight-year-old son.'

We were all hanging on to what he was saying. He was going to be OK; he only had a few weeks left to do. He looked terrible. 'I've got five kids and yeah, well, they've all got different mothers and they don't know about each other.' Five different mothers; no-one knew what to say. 'I'm going round and round trying to keep on seeing them all. I'm trying to do the right thing. I don't know how it happened. I don't.' None of us felt like taking the piss. 'What am I gonna do?'

'It could happen easy,' said Adrian, 'Course it could, these days. You wouldn't know this Al but girls nowadays, it's fucking scandalous really, the things they do.' I'd been cast as the poor old chap in the corner of the snug.

'What you do,' says Tim, 'if you're in a club for the first time, you take a look round and you find the brashest most loud-mouthed tarty looking old boot in the place and you make a big play for her.'

'What?'

'Yeah, listen. You take her home and you give her the biggest seeing to she's ever had. Do everything. Throw the fucking book at her.'

'What book?'

'You just do everything. Run yourself into the carpet.'

'What you wanna do that for.'

Tim looked round, knowingly. 'She talks to her mates. Can't keep her mouth shut she tells everybody what a fucking genius fuck you are. Goes on and on about it. After that you've got a queue forming. Can't go wrong.'

He might well have been right but I couldn't see myself trying it.

'I went on a course,' said Adrian. 'You know the sort of thing; trying to make you be responsible about sex and STDs, condoms and all that stuff. This woman running the course, she was quite nice actually, fit, she gave out some paper, big sheets of paper. She says, "I want you to write down the names of all the sexual partners you've ever had." Fair enough, I thought, why not. And I started writing away but after a bit I was thinking, "What was her name then?" I mean girls who were quite recent really. It was a bit worrying. I got half, three-quarters, of a side done. That's what? About 20? I started to feel a bit of a slag. That's what it was all for, wasn't it, crafty cow. There was this one kid he was just writing away, turned over and filled the second side. He could remember everything, names, places. Two sides full and he says to the woman: "Can I some more paper Miss?" He'd shagged hundreds and he didn't give a monkeys.'

'Yeah, well,' said Robert, 'what's wrong with that?' Robert was only a kid and you could see the way that his mind might be working. He told us about his plans for Miss World and the champagne and the limo. He looked so cheerful about the whole thing, so enthusiastic that I started to think that he might be onto something.

Then Jay said: 'That's all crap, having a woman like that sitting in the house doing nothing, can't cook, can't do nothing.'

'You have a maid for all that shit,' says Robert.

'I'd marry the maid,' says Jay.

Andrew told us about being shy. It was a very strange confession because Andrew had always spoken frankly about his sexual exploits, sometimes much, much too frankly for my peace of mind. He was close to release and he had been given a few days home leave, primarily to go into the details of a job he had been promised and to sort out his bank and just to get the feel of things. There was a certain amount of speculation about his sexual prospects.

When he came back he was unexpectedly reluctant to share his adventures. It was true, he said that his pals had fixed up a number of welcome back presents but he hadn't really wanted that sort of thing at all. In fact what he discovered was that he did not know how to behave, he was awkward, shy. 'It's the prison Al,' he told me, 'it takes all your confidence away. 'I'm shy. I've never been shy.' He looked bewildered, even the gleam of his shaven head looked embarrassed. 'I've always liked girls Al, I've never had any problem at all with girls. But now, I'll tell you, I'm tongue tied. I met this girl and I just stood there, she must have thought I was a right prawn.'

'Yeah,' says Tom, 'I got a letter from Stan and, he's the same. He says his English group is full of women but he's just like Bashful was with Snow White. He's been out weeks and no sign of legover at all.'

'Me, a shy boy. I'm not shy. Well, I am now.'

21

Yes, It's No

The Philosophy Class has been going on for about 14 years. It began in the days when there was relatively little administration, or at least not much that came my way. When Jean and Gwen persuaded me into it I said to them that I would have a go as long as they agreed that I did no administrative work of any kind. 'Of course,' they said, lying. This was one of the rare occasions when someone has underestimated me.

My advice to anyone is: don't engage at all with any of the bureaucracy. Just say no. It would go like this:

'Could I have a scheme of work from you, Alan?'

'No.'

'Well, will you do one?'

'No, no, not me'

'Lesson plans then?'

'I don't need them.'

'There's an inspection coming up, you know that don't you?'

'Good, you can send them into my room anytime. The chaps will like that.'

'But you don't have any of the paperwork.'

'I know.'

To tell you the truth most inspectors were quite relieved when I had no files or booklets or schemes and records to offer and perhaps it is only lecturers and administrators who have actually gone potty and conspired to make the bureaucratic monster which seems to be eating everything.

The thing about teaching is that there is no end to it. There is always something else that could have been discussed, some better approach, a couple of references you should have remembered. But administration—well, that's a job, a proper job that actually produces something and you can say: 'Done it.' When you have filled in all the forms, added up all the statistics, fiddled and cheated so that all the boxes can be ticked, the targets met, then you have really done a job and finished it. Teaching just isn't like that; it's never done and so it has built-in insecurity and dissatisfaction. The real purpose of paperwork in education, particularly prison education, is to give the illusion that something real and do-able has been completed—very seductive.

My advice will get you into trouble. You will have to make your way through a fair amount of flak. But get this into proportion. The flak will be, in the main, from polite middle-class liberals. Very rarely will they hit you. They might shout a bit or report you. If they shout, cry. If they report you, take comfort from the knowledge that they will be consumed with guilt and anxiety and even if they aren't, what does it matter? It's only a couple of bureaucrats being cross.

But it need not come to this. There are all sorts of ploys that you can use. The most effective is to lie. The teacher whom I personally will never forget is the colleague who taught me about the Implacable Yes. This comes into effect when you have thrown away all communications unread. If any of this stuff was—and this is extremely unlikely—important, then someone will come to see you about it. Tell them that you did it last week and sent it to their office. They will, naturally, be unable to find it. If they really—and this also is extremely unlikely—want you to do it, they will come back to you. Accuse them of losing it. Off they will go with their state of mind in one way or another disturbed. In extreme cases they will ask you to do it again. Say, yes. And then don't do it. Repeat as necessary.

Day-to-day use of the Implacable Yes avoids all sorts of tension and unpleasantness. Yes is what people want, so never give them no. You may think that I am contradicting myself here but you must remember that Yes, when it is Implacable, is only a way of saying No.

My own favourite technique was bewilderment. Everything that I was asked to do bewildered me; I was pathetic. It did not take very much of this before a woman would help me out, i.e., do it for me. 'Oh give it here,' they would say and snatch the bit of paper, delighted. I find it very odd that this cannot be overdone. Even when they know what you are up to, it still works. When someone comes along whose mission it is to get you to toe the line then you have to outlast them. It's a test of character. If you just don't do it they are, in the end, buggered. To be fair I was in a position to be able to say, 'Well then, you'd better sack me,' and follow that up with the remark that it would make a good story to tell in *The Guardian*.

The guys in my prison classes were much taken with the Implacable Yes and its variants. They had wondered why my register was stuffed with years of unanswered bits of bumph and thought that it was hysterical when I explained. But my revelation bred anxiety.

'You'd better get that register right at least, or we won't get paid,' said somebody, wagging a meaty finger under my nose. The guys were paid a small allowance for attending classes.

'Yes,' I said, 'of course I'll do it, you know I will, trust me.'

'You're doing it to us now, aren't you? That Implacable thing. Bastard. Give it here now, give me that bloody register.' And they filled it in and then shoved it under my nose. 'Check that. All right is it? Sign it there.'

I smiled.

22

Mythology and Quantum Physics, Anarchy and Erich Fromme

The new Education Block was finally built which took us out of the centre of the prison and into an isolated, fortified island. I say fortified because our new building was a single discreet block with heavily barred windows and double security doors. It was set behind a lawn, a grass moat if you like and then surrounded by high metal-mesh fences. It was now going to be a deliberate, controlled choice to come to Education. No-one, now, could wander down the central corridor on his way to work or Probation or the queue for prescriptions and just peek through the window and drop in and say: 'What you doin' in here then?' There would be no more excitement as officers dashed off to a security alert, no more of feeling a part of that busy life. On the other hand the Philosophy Class became much more calm, more stable.

There had always been a core of people who were really focused on the subject but now the whole group was drawn into being serious. Once you got to this new, isolated location there was nothing else to do, no distractions. Having everyone focussed and desperate to have their say meant that I was overwhelmed in a new way when I tried to keep order as the competition for a hearing grew more intense. Not a bad position for a teacher to be in but a part of me missed the old ways.

Cal came into the group with an heroic attitude to education. Luke had promoted him pretty heavily, 'Got to have him in the class Al; cleverest man I've ever met,' and he had been right. Cal already had a degree in Chemistry and now, in prison, he was doing an OU Physics course. He had the kind of overwhelming enthusiasm that would pull him out of his seat: 'Lemme just write this on the board,' and I would hand him the pen, slip away from the front of the class and let him get on with it. It was easy to slip into his place. Tom would hutch up a bit to give me room and Arthur would offer me a Mintoe and I could relax. Cal was quite an aggressive teacher who, unlike me, had no qualms about bollocking people for inattention or being a bit slow.

'Sometimes I think you're being fucking thick on purpose.'

Leave him be, I would say to myself, and watch. Teachers have a destructive impulse to intervene. This might be because they want to keep the lesson on track or divert trouble or maintain themselves in authority or just a prissy, middle-class desire to interfere but I had learned to keep out of things. I had grown to like a bit of confrontation and it was always interesting to see how things worked out. There might have been, sometimes, something of Tristram Shandy about the structure of my classes but that was fine, from dawn till dusk the guys already had more structure than they could sensibly cope with. From time-to-time I would cause a bit of trouble. I might lean over and let Tom tell me one of his frightening, obscene stories or flick Mintoe wrappers across the room.

'Hey, pay attention,' Cal would say, or, 'Listen to me you fuckers.' And, because he knew his stuff, we would.

'If you're going to be the teacher you shouldn't swear,' I told him.

'It's what *you* do when *you're* at the front; I'm just doing it how you do it.'

'I don't swear.'

'Yeah you do. You swear a lot. All the time.' I didn't like the sound of this at all but he was wrong, of course he was.

Tom had begun coming to classes at the same time as Cal, in fact I think that he and Cal came along together. He was one of those really intelligent men who seemed to have had almost no schooling. He was also one of the prison giants; a big muscular guy, shaven head, hands like shovels. He could look a bit severe but then, on the other hand, he could light up into a blue-eyed pearly toothed smile. He took to Philosophy like a duck to water.

Tom was like many of the guys in that he really liked the chance to sit and give his view about something, at length and without interruption. I think that this luxury is rare anywhere. Often interrupters were silenced by the other guys, 'Shut up, let him finish.' Then, it would be up to me to remember the interrupter and come back to him perhaps ten or 15 minutes later. Knowing that you would be remembered won a hearing for everyone else. Amongst other things Tom was delighted to find a whole history of thought, Anarchist thought, into which he could fit himself. Finding this intellectual pedigree was a way of making himself respectable and, because he had his wits about him, he could make those key distinctions between anarchy and disorder and between chaos and the death of authority. Like me he could see the dreadfulness of that split between the Anarchists and the Socialists at the end of the nineteenth century and how it explained, made inevitable, the descent of Socialism into centralised authoritarian structures. A very smart guy.

I liked the fact that there were no cynics in Education. Not about education anyway. Nobody gave a toss about confessing to ignorance and asking the naïve question. It was always a delight to find out just what we did know. People in prison often developed their own little specialities or had interesting pasts: mythology, nudism, wallpaper, how to cure bacon, a lot of people were experts on specialist aspects of the law. Tom might have got slightly more than he bargained for when he said that he liked science. He was sitting with Cal, and Cal sort of kidnapped him. In fact Cal arranged to transfer wings and they did some shuffling about and they ended up in next door cells so that Tom could have daily tutorials.

'Yeah,' said Tom, 'he's going to be my tutor.'

'In what?' I said, fearing the worst.

'He's going to do OU Science,' said Cal.

'What? Since when?'

'That's right,' said Tom.

'You didn't tell me.' I felt a bit put out that they'd been doing education behind my back and I was pouting.

'Don't tell you everything.'

'Obviously.'

'Will you give me a reference? Tell them how brilliant I am.'

'You should do Philosophy.'

'Science is better,' said Cal.

'For when I take over the world,' said Tom.

'Thought you were an anarchist.'

'I am. I'll take over the world and then let people do whatever they like.'

'I think that you might find,' I said, 'that people won't want that.'

'Course they will.'

'People are afraid of being free.'

'Bollocks.'

'Erich Fromme,' said Cal and away we went. 'You guys in this country are certainly afraid of being free. Herd mentality.'

'I'll make them be free,' said Tom, 'whether they like it or not.'

'Like Rousseau then.' Tom had always thought that Rousseau was a bit of a tosser and it was always a pleasure to make him jump up and down a bit.

I wrote his reference and made him sound like a close associate of Einstein and Bertrand Russell.

23

Guardians Win Koestler

It was Plato who brought Hugh into Philosophy. He had heard that there was a waiting list and so he sent in a piece of sculpture as a bid to jump the queue. It was a miniature, smaller than my thumb, of a tough kid in baggy jeans, trainers, sweat shirt, baseball cap. In one hand he held an open book in the other an Uzi. It was a lovely, intricate piece of work. Len had it wrapped up in tissue, stuffed inside a cardboard tube. He unpacked it and, very gingerly, stood it on the table.

'Don't touch,' he slapped a couple of hands away. 'You'll bust it. It's made of soap.' We gathered round, looking, our faces a few inches away from the figure.

'Guess what it is,' said Len.

'One of Plato's Guardians,' said Tom.

'Of course it is,' I said, delighted. 'I'd never have guessed that.'

'Hugh told him, on the wing,' said Cal.

'No he didn't,' said Tom, looking five-years-old.

'I've got him doing a whole set for me,' Len said. 'I'm paying him, course I am. He does all sorts.'

I've got Hugh's Guardian on the piano at home, partly because it really is brilliant, partly so that I can tell people the story. I slap their hands away and say, 'Don't touch, you'll bust it. It's made of soap.' It always makes me think, hopelessly, about Hugh.

Having Hugh in the class was a good opportunity for me to spend some time talking about Aesthetics. Everybody cared passionately about Art, especially the guys who had never had much time for it. There was something about talking about art, not art itself but talk about art, that drove people nuts. This was my secret and I used it to catch the guys unawares. They all had their prejudices and no-one had any hesitation about denouncing even slight disagreement as stupidity. It was nice to have a bit of a row now and again, it made the time fly by. This was a good thing and a bad thing; my three hour prison class tended to wipe me out and I had to spend Friday afternoons in bed. Half the class were incensed by crap that looked like nothing at all and the other half by the polka dots and body parts. Len made some mild comment about Brit Art which brought down a storm of controversy and contempt but which gave me the chance to talk about what we are doing when we call something Art. In fact I just exposed myself to a good going over

Cal clearly felt that something had to be said but, untypically, it was obvious that he didn't have the first idea what he was talking about.

'Hey if you want to put the thing I piss in on the wall and call it something that's fine. Call it what the fuck you like. It's not a word that means anything.'

And, like me, he took refuge in the way that the language of Art works. Arthur, an old-fashioned craftsman in his real life, was more inclined to talk about skill and training and spending time getting things just so. This was the view that we all had most of the time but Tom was more taken by the idea that so much money changed hands for what he regarded as crap.

'Could I do it?' he asked, looking shrewd.

'Nah,' said Len, 'you don't know the right people.'

'He'd have novelty value though.'

'True.'

Between us we covered most of the ground that you might expect in Aesthetics and when, a few weeks later, I got Derek from the School of the Arts at the university to come in, we had our ideas fairly straight, although no-one agreed with anyone else, and we were ready for him.

Derek, first time in a prison, was a bit nervous, obviously, and, at the gate, the searches and the questions about his kit for the presentation geed him up even more. If I'd warned him he'd only have worried and it wouldn't have been half the fun.

Len was first in. 'You heard about Hugh.'

'Not down the Seg again is he?'

'No nothing like that. He's won a Koestler prize.'

'What for the sculptures.'

'Yeah, course it was for the sculptures. It was obvious wasn't it? Couldn't not give it him could they?'

'Hugh,' I explained to Derek, 'makes tiny gothic figures, just a couple of inches high, gets incredible detail into them.'

'Out of soap,' said Len, 'absolutely brilliant. I was a bit pissed off actually, only got a Highly Commended for my pots. I'm better at it now though. Got next year's entry ready.'

This is all very much like normal life, the sort of conversation you might well have in Derek's department and as the rest of the guys came in and introduced themselves and shook his hand I could see him unwinding, forgetting that he was in prison at all.

Hugh could be a bit down sometimes but when he came in this morning there was a new air of confidence about him, a sort of benign false modesty in front of his public. When Derek picked up Arthur's point about the blurred areas between Art and Craft and the importance of having some business sense, Hugh said, airily, 'Yes, it's a little bit like that for me. When people ask me to do particular models for them, it might not be what I would really like to do but I have to fulfil the commission'. Hugh did his models for a bit of chocolate or a roll up.

'You know when you do your little men,' Tom began.

'My award winning sculptures,' said Hugh, 'I think that now I'd like you to refer to my work as, Award Winning Sculptures.'

'Just fucking do one will you.'

'And myself, of course, as an Award Winning Artist.'

A few of us had our heads in our hands not daring to look at the monster we had created.

Hugh had a bit of a problem, a drugs problem. Whenever he tried to beat it some unscrupulous shit would catch him a couple of days in, when he was really going through it, clucking the guys called it, and pull him back down. We all thought that Hugh was an artist, Sue in Art thought that Hugh was an artist, and he was pretty good in Philosophy. There he was, though, falling apart.

I don't know how they arranged it, maybe they found an officer who could see the sense of what they intended, but one day Cal told me: 'Hugh is living with us, me and young Tom here.' There were three of them now in a run of cells along the landing.

'Anybody comes looking for Hugh, said Tom, 'I'm there first.'

'He doesn't do anything,' said Cal, 'he's just so fucking ugly and scary.'

'I certainly am,' said Tom. Ugly might have been a bit harsh but I could see what they were getting at. It was a little bit tough having Hugh in the class; everyone thought better of him than he did of himself. We would gang up on him and tell him how good he was.

'You've got to sort yourself out,' someone would say.

'Go to Art School.' That would be me. Cal would tell him that most of the other bums had nothing to lose but that he was an artist and he had a lot to lose. Hugh would look away, half embarrassed, half angry with us for putting the pressure on him. At Easter he designed a really good product: a spring tableau with bunnies and flowers against a background of ribbons and whatever name the customer wanted to have embossed. For the market he was aiming at it was inspired. All of this was in miniature, you could easily put the whole thing on the palm of your hand, all of it was delicate.

'This guy broke his,' Hugh told me. 'He was really upset; he'd got it for his little girl. So after bang up I really concentrated on it and I stayed up and made him another one. Gave it to him first thing. He was well pleased.'

'I'll bet he was.'

'Didn't charge him. Couldn't do that, could I?'

We all felt powerless; no-one knew what to do about Hugh. Luke said that until he was ready then we might as well stop wasting our time. This was a mill that Luke had been through. I thought that he might well be right but it was bleak to find myself thinking that. I found that dealing with Hugh was difficult; he was one of a long line of men with whom I had failed. I think that failure takes its toll and there had been a lot of failure. No-one comes out of prison unscathed and when I looked at myself and how I was with Hugh I could see that prison had wormed its way in. He was such a good sculptor and yet I knew that he was going back into drug addiction. I knew it. In the past I would have discounted this, suppressed it in any account I gave of his work. Now when I sat down and talked about him with the Head of Fine Art at the university I could feel my optimism gone cold and I gave him up; I had no stomach for him. I agreed with Christine that there was no point in taking him on at the end of his sentence. He would only mess things up. My prison voice chimed in: 'Fuck him. Fuck him, what can you do?'

After he was released Cal got a letter from him; he was in love, he had stopped the heroin.

'Oh yeah, sure,' someone said, 'pussy's stronger than smack.'

There was some brief, disbelieving laughter. I was doing quite a lot of laughing now, in disbelief.

24

Naturally Good

Most Friday mornings were as bright and cheerful as you could expect in a jail. We had been talking about rights and how the language of rights threw up some interesting questions about meaning and then there was a bit of talk about nature and what Hobbes might have meant by rights which are natural to us. Fair enough. Then, the following week Cal came in with a bundle of papers: The American Declaration of Independence and the UN Declaration of Human Rights from 1948.

'Let me have a look at that,' said Ian.

'Yeah let's have a look,' said Gerard and Arthur nipped off to the office, where he had influence, to do a bit of photocopying. Then, when we had all got the documents in front of us, Cal insisted that he read out the preamble to the UN Charter and it turned into one of those mornings where all I needed to do was find the sense to keep my mouth shut.

It was a funny sort of a morning, split between deep cynicism and pugnacious optimism. Tom's view was, of course, that the main opposition to human rights, in fact to human happiness, came from governments and the sooner all government comes to an end the better.

'People,' he told us, and he sounded very confident about this, 'are naturally good and they do the right thing if they're not interfered with by those bastards.'

'That's mad,' Gerard said, 'there are people out there who'd just glass you.'

'What,' said Tom, 'are you saying that the only reason you don't attack me is because of the law?'

'I'm not saying that.'

'The reason you don't attack me is that you're a good person.' Which made us all look at Gerard in a slightly new light and then we realised that actually, yes, he was a good person which was a bit of a triumph for Tom.

Then, John got us talking about Anarchism and the Diggers and Freeborn John Lilburne and I managed to put in something about the Politics of the Deed and the European Anarchists before the First World War. Henry said that he had just had a row with someone about the war in Palestine.

'"Get out of my cell," he was saying, "get out of my cell." Really annoyed with me.'

'But you didn't hit him did you?' said Cal.

'No, course I didn't, but I didn't give in. I said something, he said something and it was okay.'

'See,' said Cal, 'you negotiated and you were sensible and you didn't need the police and the government and all that authority crap.'

'We, us, we're not free though are we?' said Gerard. 'What about the Murdoch press, they're telling people what to do, what to think.'

'If,' said Cal, 'you're stupid enough to think what Murdoch wants you to think, then fuck you.'

He and Tom had really got the bit between their teeth now and they went off on one about goodness and co-operation and freedom but then, just when it looked like they might be going to sing *We Shall Overcome*, Tom pulled a face and recoiled and wafted the UN Declaration in Cal's face.

'Have you farted?'

'I sure have,' said Cal.

'You dirty arsed bastard,' I said, seizing my chance to make some sort of contribution to the debate.

'You see, you see,' said Jed, 'that's why you need, laws, you need to keep people like him under control.'

'That's what it's like out there in the real world,' said Gerard.

'Yeah,' said Henry, 'people who just fart everywhere.'

There really is nowhere like jail.

It was hard to even begin. On my left sat the anarchists, Tom and Cal, who appeared to have lost their minds to a fantasy of human goodness. Henry was edging closer and closer to them, ready to be seduced. In front of me, Len, Arthur and Luke—laid back, cool, ready to consider the arguments. I never knew which way they were going to jump. On the right, Gerard and Jed. I was OK with their brand of realpolitik, which was always ready to do the right thing but shot through with a touch of Stalinism.

The anarchists began with a bitter denunciation of money, the centrists pointed out its utility, realpolitik its inevitability. I think this stemmed from Plato and the Division of Labour, but for Tom it was just another opportunity to make an impassioned appeal for the freedom that human goodness deserved.

Money, said Tom, always undermined freedom. Plato's denunciation of democracy was always going to lead to trouble. Tom still seemed unable to believe that, left to their own devices, people would not be intelligent and sensitive enough to behave well. His optimism was starting to get me down. I could feel the room going against me as slowly but surely Tom cast me as a miserable old fart. Jed and Gerard said some sensible things about Fascism but I let myself go off into a diatribe about the Knuckledraggers who can just about mumble and grunt their way through life.

'Ask them about prison policy, mate, all those buggers in the suburbs, and you'd all be swinging from lampposts.'

Arthur looked terribly hurt. 'Alan,' he said, 'you don't really think that people are like that, do you?' Did I? There was no backing down.

'Don't call me a Knuckledragger,' said Tom. It was a bit depressing that he thought that I'd meant him.

'Listen,' I think I might have been pointing my finger at him, 'how many people in this prison? Seven hundred? How many in Philosophy? Eight. What does that make you then? That makes you part of the elite.' Which, incredibly, shut him up.

Then he said: 'Yes, all right, guv.'

I knew what he was doing, but I was too far gone.

'Don't call me guv.'

'It's what you are though, isn't it?'

'Don't call me guv.'

'Can you nick me?'

'Certainly not.' We both knew that I was lying.

'Have you got keys?' This seemed always to be the big divide; if you had keys then you were one of them.

'I never use them.'

'How'd you get here this morning?'

'Flew. I just sort of dropped in.'

'Listen guv…'

'Don't call me guv.'

'I could call you worse things.'

Then, just when it was needed, Cal farted. He had become master of the strategic fart and I was very grateful for it. So grateful that I let him lead us back to the point. He was still particularly keen to talk about the American Constitution and I thought that I could help him out with a bit of Rousseau.

All that stuff about being born free and then being in chains was always going to cause trouble and it took us weeks to deal with and we seemed never to be any further forward. Arthur kept on saying: 'Can we get on; can we talk about the General Will?' He asked in such a polite way with his impatience only just showing that I knew that he was really wondering why I didn't get a grip and direct things. It was not so simple. Cal found this out when he started making the inevitable connections between Rousseau and the American Declaration of Independence.

'May I write something on the board,' he asked. I could think of no way of stopping him and so I gave him the pen. I think he saw the pen as power. Up he jumped and, all at once, I realised how much he looked like Rasputin. I went and sat with Tom. Cal held it together for a few minutes but then disputes about the nature of Nature broke out and my sort of chaos reasserted itself. I couldn't help but smile as he slipped into being me. 'You gonna fuckin' listen to me or not?' he snarled. Happy days.

One of the problems, not a problem really, was that Seth, who was new to the class, had the wonderful knack of asking questions. 'You've just mentioned atoms,' he said to Cal, 'what is an atom?' Quite a question, I thought, and even though it was a bit of a diversion, I resolved to keep my mouth shut. No problem, because Tom and Cal and all that OU Science were in the room and this really set them off. Seth was quite taken, and so was I, by the notion of space inside atoms and energy and the atom bomb and somehow we re-emerged into politics.

I knew that Tom would have trouble with Rousseau's imperative of forcing people to be free, even though it was exactly what he wanted to do himself, and he began his usual exposition of his Anarchist position but then the lady from the office put her head round the door.

'Could I have Tom just for a minute?' Off he went. Somehow in that split second Cal and Ade had launched into an intense and depressing conversation about neo-colonialism in Africa.

It was time that we took our break but Hugh and John pulled me into their conversation about lying. Their vehemence about politicians lying, about spin and evasion took me aback, I began to feel guilty about the easy way I had come to accept things. They clearly thought that I could do something about it all.

Tom stepped back into the room. 'You should stand for Parliament,' he said. It was somehow an accusation. 'We've got lots of mates who'd be out and about getting people to vote for you.' What mates? What did he have in mind? Forcing people to be free perhaps?

'You should get 20 years for lying,' said Hugh.

'Yeah, you should,' said Tom.

'What you got there? said Arthur.

Tom had a huge cardboard box in his hands.

'My OU stuff for the next module. It's just arrived.'

We all stood up to watch him unpack it. There were stacks of books; he just touched the covers. 'I cannot fuckin' wait to get stuck into this.'

Cal put his arm round him, 'Such a clever boy,' he said. Tom looked a bit sheepish. 'Yes you are,' said Cal, starting to take the piss.

There was a prism for splitting white light, a box of crystals. We all looked through the prism and Tom held up one of the crystals and watched it making the sunlight flicker. 'How long do you reckon it took to form this?'

'Thousand years?' said Arthur.

Tom looks at it again: 'Fuckin; hell,' he said.

Sometimes it feels like the sort of boys' public school that I used to read about in the 1950s when I was a kid; Greyfriars, with the Fifth Remove being rather cruel and innocent in the way that male exclusivity often is. Luke was obviously in a lot of pain, 'Done me knee in,' so we all took the Mick, obviously. It had taken him ages to get across the yard and then even longer to get up the stairs to our classroom.

'Playing football,' Jed said, 'for the over thirty-fives.'

'He could play for the over fifty-fives.'

'Silly old bugger.' Luke gave a little smile, rather proud of himself. At second movement he hobbled off to the doctor and we all laughed at him and sang the silly Laurel and Hardy tune. No-one dreamed of helping him, obviously. Then we turned on Len, he'd had his hair cut so he was obviously asking for it. He used to have long hair and a canvas cap now here he was with no cap and a rather nice bob.

'A bit like Audrey Hepburn,' someone remarked.

'Yeah, you can see it can't you?' Nicknames are sometimes cruel things.

What we were really interested in was Jed's day out.

'Didn't really have time for much. Had a nice lunch at the university though.' The guys take it in turn to make everything seem possible and we all felt a bit better for the fact the Open University had invited Jed to spend a day at their campus. He'd had to have a board to consider his app and in the end he got one day: out at nine-thirty, back for four.

'The wife picked me up and drove me over there. Tell you what, I was scared, sitting in the front seat and the speed of everything zipping around.'

'Fastest thing you've seen for a few years,' said Tom, 'is a table-tennis ball.'

Then they turned on me. 'Tell you what Al,' said Michael, 'You swear a lot, don't you?' which was a bit much, coming from him.

'I suppose I do,' I said, feeling a bit sheepish.

Tom looked up and said, with a voice full of regret, 'It's not very attractive, you know.'

'Attractive? I'll stop then, shall I?'

'Yeah, I would if I were you.'

'Will you be attracted to me if I stop?'

'I might be.'

'Fuckin' hell,' said Jed.

'That's a bit of self-defensive swearing is it?'

'Too right, I don't want that fucker finding me attractive.' And when you look at Tom sitting there in his vest and biceps you can see Jed's point.

We did finally get back into some Philosophy, Hobbes I think it was, and then they went back to the wings where they would be given lunch, some of them would have a nap before afternoon classes, then an early tea and into their rooms by seven-thirty. Some of them might do a bit of prep.

The guys in Philosophy knew that this was happening to them; some of them wrote about it in their OU essays. I couldn't help but think of those Billy Bunter books and wonder if the best we can do is to take away all responsibility from convicted men and then infantilise them?

25

Making History

Going into Algy's room was a trip down memory lane. Around the walls were photo-portraits of the men, some of them going back years. We always had a little bit of a wonder about what they were doing now but Algy could also tell me about how the photographs were taken, about all the false starts and failures and about how making portraits relied as much on social skills as it did on technical skill.

Kenneth had spent about 18 months doing the photography course and it had taken him over. Algy, told me how quiet Kenneth had been at first. 'This was something that he wanted to do but technically it was just too daunting. He kept on coming to class though and his pennies started dropping. I did the classic trick that always hooks people, used the light from the keyhole in the darkroom to show the guys a camera obscura, get them to realise that they're standing inside a giant camera. I try to get them to believe in photography as a way of making history, the history of their families. Photos are ten a penny nowadays, but I want these guys to take pictures that people will want to keep, something that you know has been made by an artist.'

He captivated me, never mind the men. Algy was a delicate, dapper figure, bow tie and sensitive good looks, and this only emphasised the fact that the artists in his class would look more at home in Gladiator School.

'I want them to think theatrically. I ask them, could their pictures hang in a theatre foyer and command attention like a living actor would?' Whenever I asked him about equipment he would brush the question aside.

'It's the guy behind the camera that counts, the actual kit can be as cheap as you like.

What Kenneth's learned about is people, about how to interview them and draw them out. His strength's with people and he's obviously thinking of them as individuals. A big leap that is. I was sick one week and Kenneth took the class. The maths teacher was in to supervise and he was stunned by the way the guys worked together.'

Up on the wing Kenneth showed me the pictures that he had sent to the Royal Photographic Society.

'Once the technical stuff is right I just relax and get them into conversation, chat 'em up a bit then I can get them in a natural way. I wanted to catch this bloke with the big jaw line put him right up against the wire, but that wasn't on, obviously. Security, yeah? So, I got his face emerging from the gravel, for the arrogance, got him on the upshot. This one of Alistair, I was after the constricted look in his eyes. I didn't want gangster poses. I'm looking at all sorts, films and adverts, in a different way. It's brilliant for me; I keep thinking it's a fluke, but then I keep on doing it. I've never been confident; I know I look it in what I do, but I'm not. Okay, I might have been confident in a crim way, a seedy way, but it's different now.'

'Confident?' said Algy, 'He is now. Well, they've all learned that. Confidence allows you to be patient and creative and for us in a limited environment and with limited equipment that's what we really have to have.'

One morning in Philosophy Kenneth said: 'That's it man, got letters after my name now. My mum, she's going to be so pleased.'

'What letters are they then?' Carl asked and a couple of the guys made one or two suggestions.

Kenneth turned to me: 'Nobody believes anything good do they?'

'Is it the photos?' I asked him and got the big beam.

'Yeah,' he said.

Now that Kenneth had got this Licentiateship of the Royal Photographic Society (LRCPS) and when people had seen his work they started to show trust in him. He really knew how to photograph men, but one or two of the female teachers were wondering about having portraits done and that was whole new ball game. It showed faith in him though, not just as a photographer but as a person.

'Algy's put me through all this,' said Kenneth. 'It's only when you look back that you realise how much there was to do, and I've done it. I want to do this as a living. I've been thinking about weddings and social groups. I've done a business plan with Business in Prisons: market research, accounts,

VAT. I keep on getting stuff done, but I'm ashamed of being in here. Really, you know, I am.'

I don't know how things turned out for him.

26

You'll Be a Star

Gerard was always on at me to do some Sartre. I didn't want to. I didn't know much about Sartre and I could see a mountain of work ahead of me. For some reason of his own he was worried about bad faith and he had already done a bit of the reading. He wanted to know if he'd got the right end of the stick. As far as I could tell he was doing fine and he made me promise, heart sinking, that we would spend some time on Existentialism. The group who were with Gerard were not going to be the easiest of audiences. He was the sort who made me nervous, always reading and then developing particular interests. *Being and Nothingness*, he really thought that I was going to settle down and read it.

Christine, who is in charge of something in the office, let me know that Gerard was not too far away from release but the uncertainty of things was getting him down. Not just his release date but what he was going to do. She seemed more than usually concerned and so I caught Gerard on his own before classes started. He could see what might well be the future. 'Last time, five days after I was released I was back on the crack. I want to get away from all that stuff,' he said and there was a weight of desperate resignation in his voice.

'It is, it's really difficult,' Luke said. And Luke really knows. Luke was in my class a few years ago, did his A-Levels, went off to college and now he is back. When men are released a lot of them have their clothes in a bin bag and just a few pounds in their pockets. It makes them rather vulnerable to old ways, old acquaintances.

'I'd like to do Photography,' Gerard said.

'Do it then.'

'What just like that? How?'

'Get yourself down to Algy's Photography Class.'

'There's a big waiting list.'

'If I tell him that it's urgent.'

'You reckon?'

My friend Ros worked at Colleg Harlech: an adult residential college that can access funding for board and lodging. 'Oh yes,' she said, 'we have all sorts here.' She had a long record of starry-eyed optimism but even so it seemed to be worth a try. Their photography tutor had visited the prison and seen the work that Algy did with the men and so I was hopeful. I got on the phone to their admissions office and they exceeded my expectations. There is an awful lot of 'no' in prison so that 'yes' is sometimes difficult to take. They wanted a doctor's report that Gerard was clean of drugs and some indication that he had been engaged in meaningful education whilst he had been in prison. Meaningful education? The bugger had me on my knees.

I grabbed Gerard and told him about this residential college that he could apply to and ,yes, they did the course he wanted. 'Will they have me?' he said, sounding a bit incredulous, a bit pathetic.

'Course they will mate,' said Luke, 'You'll be a star.' He gave Gerard a real boost about just how well he was going to do. Luke was worth his weight in gold.

'Where is it, Gerard asked.

'Well,' I told him, not sure how he would take to the idea, 'it's not even in the middle of nowhere. It's the edge of nowhere. Outside edge.'

'Wales mate,' Luke said. 'There's a castle.'

'I had a look at Tristan de Cunha which would have been ideal but you'll have to make do with this.'

'Is there really a castle?'

'Yeah,' said Luke, 'and a beach and then the Atlantic and then America.'

'Listen,' I said, and there was no pleasant way of asking this, 'they'll only have you if there are no drugs involved. Are there?'

He shook his head. 'Al,' he said, 'not since I got this sentence. I don't even smoke anymore.'

I did not have even a moment's doubt. If Gerard said it, then it could only be true. There was always a bit of storytelling going on in the prison. How could it be otherwise when men were locked away from reality for years, sometimes for decades? It was, anyway, something that I liked, the way that storytelling improved on truth, created a bit of drama and comedy and pathos. I sometimes do a bit of it myself. Very occasionally someone would claim to be innocent and the oddness of such a claim would always win a hearing.

When I began working in the prison I had expected everyone to be claiming innocence but this happened rarely. The conduct of the police, the barristers, the judges might have provoked comment but claiming innocence seemed to be a step too far. When Gerard gave me his word I knew that I could take it to the bank. The doctor's report confirmed this. Which left only the question of what he had been up to in Education.

As well as Philosophy Gerard was doing English, Maths, History and French and there was a lot to say about the breadth of his reading. Then, I ran him downstairs to talk to Algy about the digital film/photography course and explained that we needed to bump Gerard up the waiting list so that he could get off to a flyer when he went to college. We started saying that 'Gerard's going to college.' Sharon agreed to give him a start straightaway on the Computing Course. Then we went to see Sue in the office and asked her if she could push through the paperwork. No problem. Martin downloaded all the information so that Gerard could make his application to start his course in September. The college, after a couple of weeks said, 'Yes'. He definitely had a place.

Then Gerard vanished. 'Couple of days ago,' Len told me. 'They came for him in the middle of the morning. Couldn't get rid of him quick enough.' I must admit, I lost heart and I could quite see that he would go back to his home area meet his old pals and get back into God knows what. I went up to Probation and they told me it would be a good idea to give his outside probation officer a ring. I told her about his firm offer of a college place and I hoped that she would keep it at the forefront of his mind. Or something. I've never seen him since.

Several weeks later Ros rang up to tell me that Gerard had turned up for induction week and she phoned again at Christmas to say that he was playing a blinder, he was way ahead and why couldn't all the students be like him? 'He keeps on trying to talk to me about Philosophy of Mind,' she said. 'I don't know what he's on about.' At the end of his course he was offered a university place. He's living with his mum and doing a degree in Art. Ros says he's lovely and if only she were 40 years younger...

27

As Long as You Promise to be Really Good

It's all very well to dwell on success stories but there is a large minority of very intelligent people in prison who have to live lives which threaten them with slow destruction.

'You'd have thought, wouldn't you, that ten years would be long enough to become reasonably fluent in French?'

Barry was looking glum, arms folded, leaning forward on the desk. 'It's just not happened. All the classes are beginners' classes. I could do with being able to speak to somebody, listen to the language, get the grammar straight. Everything takes so bloody long. When I got life my Dad said that he knew I'd look after my body, but that I must, must, look after my mind.' And so, for Barry it was gym and learning French. His French class has been closed down.

It is not unusual for a lifer to spend 14 or more years in prison. This, say the psychologists, is way beyond the point where permanent mental and emotional damage is done. Many life sentences are, in effect, sentences to mutilation. No wonder, then, that prisoners can be protective about those things that alleviate the prospects of dying inside.

There are some serious students in our prisons, men who are massively read, men who have carved out niches of unexpected expertise. A lot of this study goes on in spite of isolation and limited access to books and materials. The men who are doing Open University courses invest enormous resources of willpower and determination.

During the long bang-ups of one Bank Holiday weekend, that ran in effect from Thursday to Wednesday, Keith, a lifer, had a master plan to make inroads into an essay and a pile of reading, but, up on the wing, he had run himself into the ground by Saturday. He was back in the Education

Department telling us how he would have to put himself back together, get stuck into it again.

'When I first came away I was called a murdering bastard, scum. Well, that's not all I am.' There are men serving shorter sentences who battle their way through Key Skills, GCSEs, RSAs, A-Levels; in the last couple of years we have sent men on to universities to do a range of subjects. All over the country Prison Education Departments are battling away against the prevailing culture and achieving what sometimes feel like small miracles.

These achievements should not be miracles, given the talent and intelligence that is locked up in our prisons they should be ordinary, commonplace. A way forward would be to have at least one prison which was wholly dedicated to prisoners in full-time education: a University of Prison. Such an establishment would help towards making good some of the claims about the training and rehabilitating element of imprisonment. It would also address the ethical problem of how to avoid the permanent damage, the mutilation, that comes with our current policies of long-term imprisonment. What would such a prison be like? It would be more difficult to get into than out of. It would be like a university which exacted vows of poverty, sobriety, chastity and obedience; a place where men made themselves better not worse.

We already have specialist prisons or at least sections of prisons for the insane, the geriatric, the perverted and those seeking therapy, so that the creation of an institution for those desperate to acquire an education is really not so radical. There is an enormous number of prisoners, around 86,000, they cost a fortune and many of them come back for more and more until middle-age takes the vinegar out of them. What do the rest of us get for our money? Not much. Prison cripples financially and emotionally, the loss of reputation destroys career prospects, family life and self-esteem. If we want revenge and retribution then let us have the courage to hang and flog and be done with it. Then, at least we could spend the prison millions on the Health Service. In this context the creation of a University of Prison is not outlandish it is the merest common sense. Instead of releasing men with 40 quid and a bin-bag of tatty clothes we could release at least a few hundred of them with a place in the world, a place that they would have made for themselves through work and success.

Teaching at the University of Prison would obviously be the best, most sought after job in Higher Education. The students are already the best read, the brightest, the most demanding, generous and eccentric imaginable. They already work like dogs. What they need is a community which will sustain them, give them someone to talk to. Of course there will be problems: no gap years or student exchanges, no reading weekends in the Lake District or theatre trips. There would also be the vaster problem of the spiritual parsimony of the rest of us. What a job for a Vice-Chancellor.

Keith was aware of the massive amounts of time that there are in prison, much of it spent in a ten-by-six cell.

'My mind,' he said, 'would be turning itself off light-by-light.' He mimed the switching off, click, click, at the side of his head. But why do Philosophy?

'Knowledge is power,' he said which sounded a bit odd to me.

'Power over what?'

'Just power. I'm learning about strange things, strange ways of looking at things.'

Education Sue who runs our department is struggling to keep Philosophy on the curriculum. She wants me. I can't help but feel that I'm hanging by a thread. How long will they go on tolerating Philosophy in among all those quantifiable courses, all those hours spent on Literacy and Numeracy, Health and Parenting, and Business and Computers and God knows what? Hours that count, hours that fit into the statistics, hours that Education Sue doesn't have to lie about. I feel like an illegal immigrant in education these days, being hidden by secret sympathisers from the bureaucrats who know the price of everything.

On the other hand, I can't help but feel that they, the bureaucrats, really want me, that their feelings of decency and guilt just about stop them from giving me the axe. I know the vicar wants me even though I keep on dishing out the militant atheism. He doesn't seem to mind a bit, and keeps on popping into my classes and taking the Mick and telling the guys how wonderful I am and making them smile. He knows that nothing I say to them will make a blind bit of difference.

The guys in the class want me, after all they could be off doing something useful but, instead, come to me so that we can wonder about goodness and reality and so on. They seem to take real pride in being out on a limb. A big guy in a baseball cap jumped into the room the other day, 'Can I come in Guv, just till movement?' He was looking for a hidey hole.

'Well, all right then, as long as you promise to be really good.'

'He'll be good, man,' said Arthur, 'it's Grant, course he'll be good.'

'Yeah, I'll be good,' said Grant and took off his cap, a sort of down payment. We were in the middle of a bit of Aristotle; if I had my way we'd always be in the middle of a bit of Aristotle. Flourishing: what is it that makes a human being flourish? Grant was into it in no time, seized by the idea of the Necessity of Family. When he had to go he asked, 'What's this class?'

'Philosophy,' said Arthur.

'What's that then?'

'When you asked that,' said Tom, 'you just started doing Philosophy.'

They all sat there preening themselves.

'You wanna put your name down for it,' Arthur told him.

Now Grant wants me.

And everyone still wants Pottery Sue. In her workshop you had to make a deliberate intrusion into the silence. There were four guys sitting at the modelling table, concentrating, transfixed. They took no notice of me or anything else. One of my philosophers, one of Her Majesty's Philosophers, beckoned me over to his bench. He was using a fine brush to put glaze onto a ceramic plaque that he had made. There was a phoenix.

'It's for my mum,' he said, 'I could have bought her something but it's not the same is it.' Across from him Steve has made a rough shape with a piece of clay.

'What's that?' I asked him.

'Dunno yet. I'm thinking about it as I make it.'

Michael was making a copy of a Robert Moore pot. 'For my sister. You do a lot of this for your family.'

Then Paul jumps on me. He's been listening to my foolish questions. 'It's the only thing you can do in a place like this. Course we do things for our people. Because we love them.

'See that,' he points over to the wheel where Evan is making something that looks impossibly delicate, 'he's had to learn all that from scratch.' It's a little shock to realise that the guys in this room admire each other. Pottery Sue thinks that there might not be any more money for her workshop.

The talk nowadays is all about Employability. I've given it a capital letter because people seem to think that it is a real thing in the way that we might think of God or The Promised Land as being a real thing. In its name French, Spanish, History, Literature, Art, Music, Philosophy are all in danger of being driven into the wilderness like some mangy despised scapegoat. Our managers (is that the word?) describe these subjects as 'soft' or 'fluffy.' Anything that is not Literacy, Numeracy or Computing is despised. This is how it is in prison and, I suspect, in further education generally.

Education Sue, if anyone had the wit to ask her, would make out for you a good case for the Employability value of softandfluffy. When I asked her about it she started by thinking about the plight of men who are facing long sentences.

'What's going to make them employable?'

'I don't know Sue,' she seemed to be blaming me.

'Should we just ignore them until they're within sight of release and then give them a two year dose of Employability? Fifteen years of bang up and packing shop should have put them in just the right frame of mind.' She gave the desk a good bang. 'What about geriatric prisoners? Does not being employable exclude you from the human race? Softandfluffy,' she said, 'teaches you to get up in the morning, to concentrate, to be purposeful, outward-looking, respectful. Softandfluffy addresses mental health, gives men the possibility of friendship and mutuality. And,' she said, 'and, it gives them the chance to meet strong, educated, intelligent women.'

Sue does get a bit cross about this and so, easily scared, I sat there nodding and I kept quiet about my suspicion that even she might have missed the point that some things are, simply, an end in themselves. Think of all the stuff that you really like: eating oysters, dancing, Mozart, football. Does it make any sense at all, at all, to ask what it's for? Pottery, Philosophy, Literature? No sense at all. If anyone were to insist on asking such questions you would quickly dismiss them as a nuisance, a bloody fool. Education managers not only ask these questions they demand that they be answered or else they will close us down.

I have always had a certain amount of difficulty with the world of work but I have, unfortunately, been obliged to engage with it. What I want is income, not employment. The evidence seems to suggest that this is the case for most of us. People on their way to work almost always look a bit glum; most try to minimise the amount of work they actually do when at work; breaks and lunchtimes are stretched, weekends yearned for, sickies thrown. Holidays and early retirement are what most of us want.

Work is boring and oppressive. It gets in the way of life and most of us do our best to avoid it. Of course, I know that a certain amount of it is necessary but why on earth do we pretend that it is the greatest good.

It seems that instead of teaching people about Art and History and Philosophy we have become obsessed with teaching people how to make more and more of the tawdry crap that is already choking our civilisation and making us miserable.

After Sue had given me a mauling I bumped into Luke on the corridor and I just asked him straight out why he did Philosophy.

'To move on,' he said, 'to make that leap. When you get into education you don't have to hide anymore. A lot of people hide in prison. And when people see you as bookish they can be afraid to talk to you. A guy might see me with a book and say, "What's that?" and take a look at it. Then he'll say: "Fuck that; what you reading that shit for?"'

Which is, of course, just what those who control education are saying to all of us.

28

An Incredible Lightness of Being

What I had to face up to is that I was becoming more and more indifferent and it was a difficult thing to do. There were moments, more and more of them, when I didn't care about the things that happened, who they happened to. This was the selfishness that prison rubs into your skin. I listened to what Arthur had to say, nodded the right things back at him and then shrugged him off.

Arthur led a life of growing desperation. He had an indeterminate sentence and lived from one Parole Board to the next with no real idea if release would be sooner or later. He talked to me about his wife, his children, his father and, I said to myself that if I could do anything to help him out I would. Anyone could see that he was a decent sort of a bloke. If he managed to get into the Education Block a bit early he gave our room a quick tidy, got the office vacuum cleaner and did the floor. If he caught me doing it he told me off: 'You shouldn't be doing that.' I liked him; we got on. His robust spirit was slowly winding down and sometimes he snapped at people, took refuge in contempt, laughed a lot, lot less than he used to. But, I shrugged him off. I caught myself doing it, caught myself thinking of something clever to say, making up something clever to tell myself so that I could slip away.

I had always tried to avoid this failure which began with indifference, with the feeling of, 'Oh not again,' and then justified itself with scorn. I had never tried to manage the men I met, deflect them, stand behind a platitude, promise anything and then lose the paperwork. That's the track I had started to head down towards that quiet life that I'd do anything to have. I could see it happening.

What had I thought that first morning? When Michael had said, 'I am not a criminal, I am a murderer,' what had I thought? That part of my mind which was habitually careful, intellectual, objective had met something which was unresolved, contradictory. I had walked through the gates and more and more deeply into the prison and those habits of mind had failed, eroded, vanished. There was so much to take in that all of my energy was spent in doing that; there was no space, no energy, left for making judgements. There was the luxury, not that I noticed it, of being amoral.

'There was a guy in the TV room,' said Ahmed, 'had a heart attack.'

'Oh dear,' I said, 'that must have been dreadful,' standard response.

'No,' said Ahmed, 'fucker's head had been in my way all evening, I was glad to see the back of him.'

I heard about someone stabbing a man: 'They reckon I stabbed him 47 times,' or about pouring boiling, sugary water over someone or about saving up stale piss to throw. There I was nodding and making notes. I knew that something was wrong but, just as it had been when I was a child, the wrongness had no purchase on me.

I know what to do to keep things going, sometimes when I have caught myself just going through the motions I tell myself how professional I have finally learned how to be. It's a threadbare attitude. What I want to say is: 'Just behave yourself, it's not that difficult. Keep away from drugs, don't hit people, don't steal. Don't do it. What good is that? I founder, what else would I do, on the prison's lazy cynicism and I think about Larkin's 'cast of crooks and tarts' who run the country.

Before I know where I am I begin to tell myself a story.

'If I were in my twenties, I could do five years, easy. If I were in my twenties I would go into the drugs business and make a fortune. Boxes of ready money under the sink, buy paintings and antiques, salt it away ready for when I get out. I could have done five years, well, three, when I was 20.' It's easy to lose sight of the simplicity of being good; easy to make up excuses for the wrongness. Never mind the crooks and tarts that's their business.

It was important for me to remember that being a teacher in prison placed me among prisoners rather than amongst criminals. Many of them were as disturbed as I was by the prospect of criminality. Men like Michael went to great lengths to preserve a vision of themselves where there was honesty and respectability. But, being a prisoner, for whatever reason, is a distinct way of being. It is, obviously a restricted state and these restrictions alter the boundaries of what it is to be a person.

A lot of the men I met had left behind, in many cases had lost forever, job, house, car, wife, children, status. Imprisonment in our society is a radical, piercing punishment. Many of the men were stunned by this new lightness of being, made desperate by anxiety, nauseated by the moral, social freefall in which they found themselves. The men I met were often intelligent, reflective people and this made things better and worse. If they weren't then it was my job to make them intelligent, reflective, better and worse.

This perspective, what my job was, was lost. I lost it in the routine of doing something which was, for the most part, beyond me. The routine, the moral routine of the prison, wormed its way into my head and I resolved to be free of it. I began trying to allow myself to stop doing this job. But, I felt obliged. There were people in my class who had been there for a couple of years and it was not possible to just turn away. In however peculiar a way, we were friends and you don't just walk away from your friends. Of course prison friendships are mostly temporary affairs.

There are rules which govern what should happen when prison is over and if I did run into people on the out I felt more comfortable if there were some kind of academic, professional framework. I think, too, that no-one likes to be reminded of prison. For me, though, right now I want to leave. It's been 14 years and I feel a bit knackered. This Friday I did my class and then, in the afternoon, as usual, I went to bed. I didn't have a nap; I went to bed. In the evening I went to see the Saints play, back in bed for eleven and slept like a log.

'Why do you let me sleep so much?' I asked my wife.

She grinned: 'Oh, I think I've realised you're getting old.'

'My wife says I'm old,' I told Arthur.

'How old are you?'

'Sixty-four.'

'Fuck, yeah,' said Wolf, 'that is old.'

'Bastard.'

'But you don't look it.'

'No you don't,' said Arthur, 'Not really.' But, the damage was done.

I made up my mind to leave. 'What I'd like to do,' I tell Sue, 'is not to have any new students. A few men have left recently and I'm down to four anyway. Just don't send me anyone new, just let the class fade away. I know

it's not a viable class and all that nonsense but you don't have to pay me.'
It was a way of making running out of steam sound a bit more respectable.

Back in my room, Ben had turned up. Don't ask me from where.

'We've been playing chess,' Cal told me, 'and we just need to catch up.'

They didn't have any chessmen. All they had was a rough sketch of a
chessboard that Ben had drawn on a piece of A4. They sat there mumbling
to each other.

'So, what takes the bishop?'

'The castle.'

'Oh yeah, right.'

They had been playing chess in their heads, sending the moves via third
parties from I Wing to C Wing. Ben hung around listening to us talk about
emotive meaning and cognitive meaning and he was still there at the end
of the morning.

'Can you write me in the register,' he said, 'or I won't get paid.'

The class was fading away from four to five. How could you turn him
away, he plays chess in his head and asks questions about how words come
to mean things? There was no way out and the damned class was growing.
Another guy dropped in.

'Who are you then?, I asked him.

'That's Ten Foot,' Cal said. There was no reason to ask why.

'I should be in computers, they won't miss me' (they did and he was in
trouble). Ten Foot was worming his way in, knew a soft touch when he saw
one. At this rate there would be 12 of them by Christmas.

29

Go Into the Hardest Pub in Town ...

Andy had been in Prison Education for about 30 years and he ought to have been a bit worn out, a bit cynical, but he wasn't. No-one was, not even me, not really, and I just couldn't see why not. After all the guys seemed to do a fair bit of fouling up; they got put into Seg, messed up parole, re-offended, got another sentence.

At his retirement do at the local Italian he treated us all to the usual terrible jokes and then fell to musing about the possibilities of an Old Boys' Association which might well have been one of the terrible jokes but he was so far gone in optimism that he could just have meant it. After all, he said, other colleges have them so why not us? Could there be a corner of Friends Reunited for our guys. Would it be legal?

All of us wondered what became of people when they left and from time-to-time a letter dropped into the department that brightened up the day. One man's mother wrote in to say thank you for making sure that her son got into university. He'd gone out one Friday evening for a drink with his pals and ended up with six years after a fight went far too far. A longish weekend, which made me think how lucky I had been as a young man to avoid that fate.

Then we heard that Frank had become a plasterer, got married, had a baby to look after. Rory had become a carer working with adults with learning difficulties. Another guy had graduated with a good degree in Philosophy. It wasn't all gloom, not by a long way. The Open University is good at getting a grip on people and presents our students with good, solid proof that they can succeed. They have to reassess what they can do.

'Not for me,' Jared said, when I started to nag him. 'I'd have to say that all my schoolteachers were right and I was wrong and I'm not about to do that, now am I?' He got into his OU course but he told me that he had to do it as a series of cliff-hangers, had to leave everything to the last minute and then have a fraught weekend without sleep to hit his deadlines. I think he liked a crisis. He'd been going to classes with Luke who was a bit of an OU star.

'He's bloody good Luke is,' he told me, quietly.

'I know he is Jared,' I said, 'so are you.'

'Yeah, well,' he said and looked a bit awkward.

Andy finally finished his speech and ordered everyone another drink and Sociology Carole said, 'I wonder what Big's doing and then we sat and wondered about Eddy and Simon and Patrick and Len.

I don't know why Eddy drifted into Education, he didn't seem the type. Then he found that Shakespeare was easy, *Henry V, Macbeth* and Blake and Yeats and Heaney, anybody good in fact. There are lots of guys like this and being with them in class is just surreal. Go into the hardest pub in town and start a conversation about Wordsworth. Go on, I dare you.

I sat there with Andy and had a few drinks and thought about Cal and Arthur. Cal had excused himself from a class. 'I'm going to the Offender Management Unit, sorry, I'll try to get back if I can. What was there to say to Cal in that unit. I'm sure that they dreaded him turning up; everything you could recommend him to do he was doing. Afterwards he said, 'Oh they just told me to keep on doing what I was doing. It'd be nice to make some progress with them though. You know, get my D Cat or a date for a Parole Board hearing. It's been more than six years now.'

I had to admire his resilience, and I have to wonder how much more there is of it.

'There's this,' he showed me an inch thick manuscript, 'and this,' slapping them down on the desk. He's involved in two legal campaigns, publishing papers and doing his degree. 'Then there's this,' and there were more documents and clippings which related to Arthur's situation.

'I'm a bit worried about Arthur,' I told him. 'You can see he's getting a bit snappy.'

'Yeah,' said Cal, 'Arthur is a worry.'

Some people are in prison for not very long, some are too dull to be seriously damaged but Arthur did not have a release date and he was an intelligent man who could see what was happening to him and could see too that he could not stop it. Prison was making things worse and worse.

I worried about Cal. I worried whether he could hold together the busy, intellectual, tough guy persona that he had made for himself. I was used to him meeting me head on, transparent, good natured, full of ideas and enthusiasm; I feared that he might begin to slide behind a screen of irony and then sourness and then, worst of all, defeat. He was one of those men who relieved me of any anxiety about morality or justice. I just wanted him to be okay; get himself through it, intact, like Charles did or Gerard. No bitterness, optimistic, full of work and goodwill.

After class one morning Cal came back into the room.

'You okay?' he said.

'Yeah fine. I'm alright,' but I wasn't.

'It was an upsetting morning,' he said. 'I feel upset myself.'

'Tell you what Cal, if I never meet another psychopath again as long as I live, it'll be far too soon.' And I knew that I had lost the stomach for the whole damned business. If I carried on in prison then I would have to do it differently; I would have to admit that it was prison. In 14 years I had never excluded anyone from my class no matter how difficult they were, never given a nicking, no matter what, never turned anyone away. It had all been a bit of a club where everyone was good and bright and sensitive, especially when they weren't. But now, standing in the corridor with Cal, they could all just fuck off.

Teaching in a prison means that from time-to-time someone who is really difficult walks through the door. I always felt obliged to persist, not to simply chuck them out. 'You can't treat people like that,' I would say when the guys advised me what they would do to the current nutter. Now, I had started to agree with them and it felt like failure. My bottle had gone and I wanted to get under the duvet and stay there. There was a whining voice nagging away inside offering me a sour commentary on what I imagined my classes were about.

Cal gave me a hug, slapped me on the back: 'Retire, man. You don't need all this shit.'

After almost 14 years, it really was time to go. I couldn't just walk away, just leave the guys flat. I offered them a deal. I would stay as long as they did. There was a certain amount of dark laughter. 'You might have a long wait.'

And then, out of the blue, there was a run of golden, other-worldly mornings when we read Chaucer. Chaucer. It started when Ten-Foot thought I was kidding when I said that there was a Marxist account of language. They couldn't get enough of the Canterbury Tales, that lovely run of characters. It cheered me up to know again that anything good, no matter how old, obscure or difficult, always commanded a hearing.

We took our time over the spelling and where words might have come from or gone to. I told them about David Crystal and the notion of polite rather than correct English. We really got into it. The men's enthusiasm reassured me that I hadn't wasted my time. What after all does education offer to people if not a greater sense of being human. When we don't know about History and Art and Society we are adrift, vulnerable to the next charlatan. Most of you reading this will never have had that experience but many of the men I taught were ignorant of just about everything and as grown men felt this keenly. Education was a relief, a route to self-respect.

For the most part classes in the Arts, Social Sciences, languages have been closed. There won't be much of my liberal nonsense in the future. The government have decided that training for work is the way to go and, for the most part, education, beyond basic numeracy and literacy, has been abandoned. I can't see it myself. Of course there are men for whom training is just the thing and it will succeed. But, in prison nothing succeeds for everyone; prison is an enormously diverse place. In my classes there were men who were mad, addicted, beyond retirement age. There were men whose intention was to go straight back into crime. There were men who were feckless or alienated or simply bewildered. There were of course sensitive, intelligent men who had decided on higher education. So, anyway, good luck with the training.

Then, Ten-Foot was gone.

'Released,' Cal told me.

'He never said he was due.'

'Some guys don't,' said Cal.

'Yeah, I know, I know.'

Then, Arthur went. I'd appeared at his parole hearing and been at a loss how to make them understand what a good bloke he was. Everybody there said he was. We were all desperate for them to say, yes.

It was just me and Cal and I had the full, unrelenting blast of his enthusiasm for everything. I also got all of his thrilling adventures which had landed him so badly in the soup. I told him some stories of my own, about that first class.

'I am not a criminal,' Dean had said, 'I am a murderer,' and it had taken me years to understand.

I told him about Charles who had left prison to go to the LSE, Malkie the Glaswegian yogi pool shark, Pete the Nudist, Budgie Blue Legs and on and on. I had been really fortunate with the men who lingered on, intelligent civilised men who clung on to respectability.

In the end it was me and Cal. We decided to do Quantum Physics, he had the maths for it, and for a few months we followed a course of lectures on CD. I know that I tried his patience, making him go over things three or four times but he was a good teacher.

One afternoon Sue rang me up at home, 'Cal was shipped out yesterday.' And I was finished.

Index

H

I

J

Mary Ann Cotton: Britain's First Female Serial Killer

by David Wilson

Mary Ann Cotton is not just the first but perhaps the UK's most prolific female serial killer, with more victims than Myra Hindley, Rosemary West, Beverly Allit or male predators such as Jack the Ripper and Dennis Nilsen. But her own north east of England (and criminologists) apart, she remains largely forgotten, despite poisoning to death up to 21 victims in Britain's 'arsenic century'. Exploding myths that every serial killer is a 'monster', the author draws attention to Cotton's charms, allure, capability, skill and ambition—drawing parallels or contrasting the methods and lifestyles of other serial killers from Victorian to modern times. He also shows how events cannot be separated from their social context—here the industrial revolution, growing mobility, women's emancipation and greater assertiveness.

Paperback ISBN 978-1-904380-91-7 | 224 pages | 2013

WatersidePress.co.uk/MAC

Murderers or Martyrs

by George Skelly, Foreword by Lord Goldsmith

A spell-binding account of an appalling miscarriage of justice. Charged with the 'Cranborne Road murder' of Wavertree widow Alice Rimmer, two Manchester youths were hastily condemned by a Liverpool jury on the police-orchestrated lies of a criminal and two malleable young prostitutes. George Skelly's detailed account of the warped trial, predictable appeal result courtesy of 'hanging judge' Lord Goddard and the whitewash secret inquiry will enrage all who believe in justice. And if the men's prison letters (including from the condemned cells) sometimes make you laugh, they will make you weep far longer.

Paperback ISBN 978-1-904380-80-1 | 480 pages | 2012

WatersidePress.co.uk/MoM

Amin's Soldiers:

A Caricature of Upper Prison

by John Pancras Orau

Following the fall of African dictator Idi Amin, remnants of his army were rounded-up and thrown in jail. John Pancras Orau, a member of Amin's Ugandan Air Force was one of these men. He saw first-hand the privations, isolation, hunger and humiliation in what were little more than concentration camps. In this book he describes the uncertainty and arbitrary punishments that — alongside fear that prisoners might just 'disappear' — were part of daily life. A true story of hope and belief, Amin's Soldiers is a masterpiece in tragicomic writing falling somewhere between *Catch 22* and *Animal Farm*.

Paperback ISBN 978-1-904380-96-2 | 190 pages | 2013

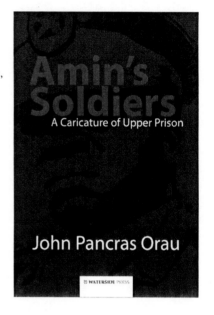

WatersidePress.co.uk/UP